Evans Modern Teaching

History with Juniors

Evans Modern Teaching

History with Juniors

Michael Pollard

Evans Brothers Limited   London

Published by Evans Brothers Limited
Montague House
Russell Square, London WC1

Filmset in 10 on 11pt Imprint by
Thomson Litho, East Kilbride, Scotland,
and printed in Great Britain by
T. & A. Constable Ltd., Edinburgh.

ISBN 0 237 28845 1   PRA 3190

0049983

Contents

Chapter 1

Starting with yesterday

This book is based on the view that—at any rate so far as junior and middle school children are concerned—history has traditionally been taught the wrong way round. In other words, we should begin at the end with the study of yesterday.

Although this thesis is unlikely to be as startling as it might have been a few years ago—teachers have become familiar with the sight of the traditional syllabus standing on its head—it nevertheless needs some justification. This can easily be found in the record of what history teaching has and has not done for our pupils.

Large numbers of children, taught history in the traditional way, have become familiar—often several times over during the course of their school lives—with the most intricate technical details of how Stonehenge was constructed, of the conditions of apprenticeship and journeymanship in the late Middle Ages, and of the day-by-day tribulations of the early world explorers. Many can describe accurately according to their sources, though not always accurately according to historical truth, the costume, domestic furnishings and architectural detail of various periods. Traditional history teaching has, however, failed to tell them how their own city or country surroundings have changed in the present century, or even during their own lifetimes; or how trade unionism has altered the working lives of their fathers; or why perhaps their own families, originally from the country, have now settled into town life. When history stopped being a matter of lists of dates—wars, battles, treaties and monarchs—it became more interesting, but not necessarily more relevant.

We often hear about the rate at which the frontiers of knowledge are being pushed back, and it is usual, in this connection, to think of science—and perhaps of geography, now that a space atlas is becoming as essential a reference book as a terrestrial one. It is as well to remember that history, too, expands—daily. For some of us, it is sobering to find that history books are now being produced about events we remember reading about in the daily papers as news. But it is not merely that the list of happenings in the story of man in the world is getting longer. The speed with which one event succeeds another is increasing, too. A fairly recent example of this was the Six Days' War between Israel and the Arabs in June, 1967. In terms alike of the terrain covered, the scale of casualties and damage, political consequences or any other yardstick one cares to choose, the Six Days' War bears comparison with many a campaign in any of the centuries before the eighteenth which might have gone on for years.

It is not only in international affairs that the increasing pace of change can be observed. When the Church was the focal point of social as well as spiritual community life, churches were built to last, and few places in Britain are far away from a church which has been standing for hundreds of years. It would be true to say that in the 1930s the cinema became the focal point of social life in most towns of any size, and the boom in cinema attendance resulted in the building of super-cinemas by such circuits as Odeon, Gaumont and Granada. These buildings had a distinctive style of architecture, and dominated the High Streets in which they were built. Yet already—less than forty years later—many of them have outlived their usefulness and have been demolished to make way for supermarkets, office blocks, car parks—the trappings of another stage in the social revolution. In the renewal of the centres of our larger cities, we have embarked upon a process which could conceivably go on for ever, because these centres are not so much being built anew to bring them up to date as in a state of constant flux to keep them abreast of constantly-changing social, commercial, industrial and community needs. If history has anything to offer to children, it is the reasons for these changes. If we are to make history as relevant to children as we are striving to make other areas of the curriculum, we must do so by relating it to their world. For this reason, if any part of history is to be omitted in school—and clearly something must be left out if we are to deal with anything at all adequately—I should prefer it to be, say, the civilisation of Ancient Egypt rather than the events which have shaped the day-to-day lives of the children we teach.

And not only, to be sure, the children we teach. I live in Chiswick, west London, roughly half-way between the point where Caesar is said to have crossed the Thames in 54 BC and the site of the old Chiswick Empire, which was pulled down in the 1950s to make way for a supermarket. I don't think it is entirely a matter of personal taste that I find the second fact more interesting than the first. The fact is that I have a reasonable chance of getting into secondhand contact with the heyday of the Chiswick Empire. As it happens, it was the venue for my wife's first visit to the theatre at the age of five, but apart from this there are plenty of other points of contact.

There are enough theatres of the late music hall era still standing for me to go and have a look at one of them. There are songbooks and records which give a good idea of the flavour of the twice-nightly bills. I could see collections of playbills, programmes, theatrical photographs and other relics. And although the one great disability to which all students of history are subject is still true—I can't be *there, then*—I can get closer to the *there, then* of the Chiswick Empire than I can to the day Caesar crossed the Thames. Here, I stand no chance at all. The only image I can bring to mind, if I visit the site, is of the centurions marching across the rooftops of Barnes and re-forming again, after the crossing, in the terraced streets to the west of Hammersmith —an unsatisfying picture.

Until recently, these views would have been heresy to most teachers of history, and even now, I'm sure, they will seem fairly extreme to some. One of the fictions that history teaching has been at some pains to create and sustain is that time's winged chariot has been driven without a break, and in a direct line, from the civilisations of earliest recorded or re-discovered history to today. This view is typified by Dr John Fines, who, writing in the introduction to a teachers' source book on history,[1] asked: 'How better could we explore problems of vandalism and gang warfare than in considering the careers of those two mighty gangsters, Marius and Sulla? Who can teach us better about problems of honesty and conscience than Martin Luther in dispute with Erasmus?' These questions may be tenable—though I doubt it—in Dr Fines' college of education, but they are unlikely to be of much help to the teacher faced with the challenge of teaching history in downtown Birmingham, Liverpool or Shepherd's Bush. It seems to me that the only problems explored in history which can reveal much to present-day children— or adults, for that matter—are those in which an immediate analogy can be drawn with today's problems and conditions; and analogies between either Reformation Europe or Classical Rome and today are hard to find. There is still faith in some quarters, however, in the lessons of the distant past, and when I challenged Dr Fines' words, quoted above, in a review of his book he replied, with both conviction and wit, that my 'vision of ridding the nation of its monuments and museums (while perhaps retaining one amphitheatre where teachers may see the children of Sparkbrook mauling a succession of weak and feckless college lecturers) has a certain charm, but it would not, I feel, advance the cause of teaching far.' True, true; but neither—and this is, in a sense, the message I want to get across in this book—would it do history teaching much harm.

[1] *History,* edited by John Fines. (Blond Teachers' Handbooks, 1970.)

At school, I was taught history up to 1914, which was where the textbook stopped; and even then the period since 1899 was covered in an extra chapter tacked on to the original edition. Looking back now, it seems that the fifty years preceding 1914 were covered pretty thinly. A bright, cynical child, which I was not, might have formed the conclusion that this was because historians had not yet made up their minds what to think of them. Over the whole of my school career, however, there seem to have been a number of densely-woven patches — around, for example, 3000 BC, 55 BC, AD 1066, and so on. I used to wonder, in 1948, why history appeared to stop short at 1914 — a year when *real* history, as opposed to the processed school product, seemed to have started for my parents and grandparents. As I liked the subject, I felt a bit hard done by — sold short, as it were. Later, however, I was to realise that I was particularly fortunate among my generation, and even among succeeding ones, to have got as far as 1914. My contemporaries and many of my successors stopped even earlier; 1870 or the turn of the century seem to have been popular historical finishing-posts.

I am writing now of GCE A-level candidates. If we look at the experience of pupils who do not get that far we find the gap between history and reality even more marked. It is true that in many CSE courses some enlightened teachers are taking such topics as nineteenth-century social history, or industrial archaeology, for course work, but even here there are some dangers. Unless children are given some kind of base on which to set the figures they discover in the course of topic studies, nineteenth-century events, close as they seem to us, can all too easily float in the mists of time as buoyantly as such traditional themes in history as the Civil War or the story of the Princes in the Tower. But this is the problem of relatively few children. Much school history is still of the more conventional sort, and fails to make even a token attempt to link past and present. Much of it, I'm tempted to think, is based on the principle that the longer ago something happened, the better its historical *bona fides*. How else can one explain the disproportionate concentration, out of all world history, on a limited number of ancient history topics?

This limitation is particularly noticeable in the typical junior and middle school syllabus. The fact is that since we abandoned the practice of committing rote lists of dates to memory — a procedure which must, I reluctantly suppose, be regarded as history teaching of a sort — we have not taught *history,* in any meaningful sense, to children outside CSE and GCE courses. What we have substituted is the antiquarian appreciation of the past, an amateurish study which requires little from either the teacher or taught. Just as teachers of the late nineteenth century, unable to cope with the teaching of science and unable to afford the equipment to do so, invented the pseudo-subject *nature study* which demanded no apparatus and little knowledge or ability beyond mere observation, so the teaching of history, I fear, has been diluted to a sort of vague study of relics, bolstered up at the lower end of the junior age-range with woolly and unhistorical story-telling.

Some of this story-telling is, indeed, not so much unhistorical as anti-historical. It is still possible to find in use—and even newly-published—'story approach' history sets for the junior school in which Middle Ages characters converse in Gadzookery, and Stone-age children (in spite of the fact that they may have names like Og and Ith) speak in the unmistakable language of 1930s Surbiton. It is surprising that teachers who would regard the works of certain popular historical novelists as meretricious trash expose their pupils to fictionalised history no less inaccurate and worthless.

The attempts of some teachers to lend authenticity to the study of relics by taking their classes to view the remains can meet with scarcely greater success in terms of effective history teaching, though they may have resulted in many a happy day out of the classroom.

Children who have been studying the Roman conquest of Britain, for example, are taken by the coachload to St Albans. When they get there, they see the reconstructed theatre, looking now not very much as it did when it was in use, together with a number of areas of gravel outlined by concrete coping-stones and labelled *wine store, kitchen,* and so on. The shrine on the theatre site is a concrete pit which could just as easily be a drainage sump installed last year by the St Albans Corporation. Small wonder that, driven miles across country to inspect putative remnants like this, large numbers of children leave school thinking of history as either a confidence trick or some game invented by adults for their own amusement but which requires a number of children as players.

The effort of imagination required to 'get anything out of' a visit to most ancient monuments is something beyond the capacity of children—certainly at junior school age. These visits could be justified as part of the history curriculum—I say nothing of justifying them in other terms, though in fact any school outing probably does justify itself, somehow—if only it were possible to get from ancient monuments at least a whiff of the scent of what it must have been like to live there at the appropriate time. I know of very few where you can get even this, a possible exception—though this is probably an adult and personal judgment—being Avebury, seen from the long avenue towards West Kennett in late afternoon in winter.

Too easily, visits to monuments, like historical story-telling, can become anti-historical. We soak our classes in the story of Stonehenge, making use of the many excellent visual aids available, and then destroy our pupils' belief in us—maybe for life—by taking them to see it—a remarkably unimpressive collection of refashioned and reconstituted stone on a Wiltshire hillside which it shares—to the detriment of the visitor's capacity for awe—with an army camp and a large road junction.

Or we go in search of relics on a more modest scale and nearer home in the local museum, again straining our pupils' respect for us as teachers. We take them along to see bits of stone and pottery which look much like bits of stone and pottery they might dig up in their own gardens or on a waste site, but which date from rather longer ago. Or we embark upon a project about the local church, ignoring the fact (because many of us aren't aware of it) that it is almost impossible to relate any pre-Victorian church interior to its environment because of the passionate and vandalistic 'restoration' in which nineteenth-century parsons indulged. Small wonder that history becomes, for most people, a museum culture, and that our national monuments become little more than picnic parks with a cultural gimmick.

Traditional history teaching owes a great deal to the Victorians' perception of the world and Britain's place in it. Charlotte M. Yonge concluded the 1884 edition of her *Stories of English History for the Little Ones*—a greatly respected textbook of the time—thus: 'History is being made from day to day, and when we have come down to our own times, we ourselves are the people who make the honour or dishonour of our country, by the way we live, the habits we form, and the part we take in all that is going on.' This was a reasonable and unimpeachable criterion for teachers of history in late Victorian England, when it was customary to see the nation as the setting of a long pageant—and Miss Yonge and other educational historians of the period could make it seem very long indeed—of kingship, battle, conquest, victory and, more recently, reluctant social reform.

How each age sees itself is its own affair, and it would be unbecoming of us to sneer at the Victorians; the more so as we live in an age which may well be seen by later generations—if they are here to see it at all—as either incredibly repressive or foolhardily liberal. But the national awareness which was the main plank of Miss Yonge's approach to history faded progressively from 1914 onwards, and disappeared altogether after 1945. We have not replaced it as a basis for history teaching by anything as clear-sighted. In 1884, the teachers, if not the taught, could feel a direct relationship between any period of English history after the Conquest and their own time.

What we teach now as history cannot be based on that sense of a direct relationship, and in the absence of a substitute it seems to have degenerated into little more than a sentimental affection—not even reverence—for the past which has no real roots in felt experience. It is salutary to reflect that in recent years the producers of television documentary programmes and films, and the publishers of part-works, have joined the writers of historical romances in making history more attractive and acceptable to the general public than even the best history teachers.

If there had been a Nuffield project on history, or if the Schools Council had devoted one of its major studies to the subject, things might have been different. The fact is, though, that history has become a Cinderella subject, unloved by school-leavers, good for examinations in secondary schools but little good for anything else, and too easily swallowed up anonymously in those unallocated areas of the junior school timetable. A curriculum development programme on history would, however, doubtless have drawn upon the same source of inspiration as informed the Nuffield maths and science schemes—the Piagetian proposition that children should begin by studying topics close to their own experience and should then move out concentrically in a process of discovery, just as they do in geography by looking first at their own homes, then at their own streets, then at their own towns, and so on until they reach the study of the world as a whole. Adapting this principle to history, it seems reasonable that children should begin their studies not with civilisations with which they can feel no contact at all but with the area of history which is closest to them—their own and their parents' time.

The concept of time—past or future—is one of the most baffling that young children meet in early life. It is the more difficult because it cannot be made clear by the use of apparatus, as can the almost equally baffling concepts of mathematics, or by practice, as with concepts involved in the reading skills. Even educated adults suffer to some extent from the same difficulty; it is not easy to gauge one's relationship in time with the eighteenth century, still less with Ancient Mesopotamia. But adults acquire a set of mental yardsticks which at least give an illusion of accurate relative time-measurement: *before the war, in Victorian times, in the Middle Ages, before Christ.* In fact, probably very few of us, unless we have studied the period academically and in detail, have a clear idea of when the Middle Ages were, or could give an adequate summary of the society, politics, religion, literature, culture and economics of the time—but this doesn't stop us using the term *Middle Ages* as a piece of historical punctuation, as a peg on which to hang such assorted bits of knowledge as we may have.

Children have no such aids at their disposal. We use the term *before Christ,* to take another example, as if it were as easy to understand as today's date. We assume all too easily that the most obvious and clear-cut distinction in historical time is that between the dates before and after the birth of Christ. Children have, of course, no cultural tradition to support them when we postulate this; for them, the BC/AD concept is as mysterious as the Chinese calendar is to the rest of us. To make matters worse, there is the added complication that dates BC are in descending order, and they have been tacked on to events only in hindsight.

Our glib use of BC and AD is typical of the difficulties which history presents to children, and characteristic of the traditional sub-academic way of teaching history which has been allowed to grow up in schools. We graft historical terms on to time without thinking, forgetting that the Middle Ages were not the Middle Ages when people were living through them, that only post-Victorians have learned to speak of the Victorian age because only they were to discover how definitively it was to end with the Queen's funeral, and that only after the Second World War did people start to speak of the First World War instead of the Great War.

Some years ago, it was fashionable to try to solve the time-concept problem in schools with charts which showed, say, the building of the Great Pyramid at one end and the building of the Royal Festival Hall (hardly in the same class) at the other. This was a well-meant but ineffectual attempt to bridge the cultural gap between adulthood and childhood. Of course, time-charts have their uses in showing a sequence of events over a limited period of time—say, the causes or progress of a war. But they do nothing to give a child a scale by which to measure history as a whole. Presenting a child with a time-chart is like presenting a traveller in an unknown country with a map from which the scale and key are missing.

This, then, is another reason for starting the teaching of history from this end. It doesn't seem to me to matter that, following this through, children may not, in the junior school, look back more than, at the most, two hundred years—and probably a lot less. They will, in the process, have found out something about historical method; they will know something about what sources are available for historical study; and they will have at least some idea of scale to help them when they venture further back into the past.

There is also this. What is the object of teaching history? It is a little high-sounding but nevertheless generally true to say that one of the objects is to acquaint the young with their national traditions. This was Charlotte M. Yonge's concern in 1884, and although our view of what our national traditions are has changed (or been changed for us by national misfortune) it is still a reasonable enough aim. And it is true of history teaching in other countries. Those of us who have watched American education in action may have felt somewhat stifled by its obsession with the early constitutional history of the United States. But the American constitution is so closely linked with American law and institutions generally that the place it occupies in education is not as unreasonable as it might be if we were, in Britain, to devote the same amount of time to, say, Magna Carta. Our own national traditions are rather more woolly; the insularity of the British, for example, is some-thing which can be directly traced back through history. But most of the elements which make up our national consciousness—or perhaps un-consciousness—are of more recent origin; folk-memories in Britain are of the slump of the 1930s (check this is any northern industrial town), of the Blitz (check this in east London), of the traumatic shock of the sinking of the Titanic (check in Southampton, where the crew came from). In this situation, children will get more help from a study of the present century than from tinkering with the truth about ancient civilisations.

It has become a truism that life has changed more substantially since 1900 than in the whole of previous recorded history. There seems little point in taking children back through time to the ancient civilisations or even to pre-history when there are, much closer at hand, periods to study which are, in real terms, only minimally less remote: when night was unrelieved by electricity, when travel was a rare luxury, when the only sounds in the world were first-hand ones, not recorded or electronically transmitted, and so on.

Similarly, local history for the junior school is less a matter of when the church was built and whether any local relic was mentioned in Domesday Book than of what the fields were like before the by-pass and the new estate were built, what the shops in the High Street used to look like, and 'what it was like when Mum was a little girl'. This approach follows all the canons of pedagogy, like proceeding from the known to the unknown, starting with experience, and so on. It is an approach which, as will be seen, suffers from no shortage of easily-available source material. And it is an approach which, while stretching the intellectual capacity of the ablest children quite far enough, provides scope within which everyone can work on the particular segment of history which is of most importance, relevance and interest to junior and middle school children.

Chapter 2

Family affairs

It is impressive to reflect on how well-equipped a reasonably well-educated adult is to measure the national and international events of his lifetime, and sometimes even his own personal experiences, against historical precedents. We do this constantly, often unconsciously. When, in the 1960s, General de Gaulle was being obstructive about Britain's entry into the European Economic Community, he appeared, to the average British mind, to be playing out a role common in the Anglo-French drama throughout history; the General merely confirmed to many British people the conviction, born of learning about the French Revolution and Napoleon and the repeated troubles of nineteenth-century France, that nothing but unhappiness and possibly disaster could be expected of trying to shake hands with the French. To take another example, the policy of Soviet Russia in the Middle East can be traced back in a direct line and without too much difficulty at least to the Czardom of Peter the Great. Contemporary attitudes on the employment of women and young people owe a great deal to what we have learned about female and child labour in mines and factories in early Victorian times and before. Our reaction to the monthly official unemployment figures is coloured by memories of the slump of the 1930s—though the number of people with first-hand memories of that time is dwindling. And so on.

One of the main purposes of learning history, in fact, is that it enables us to order our ideas about the world in which we live, just as a knowledge of science helps us to interpret another set of experiences. This is a powerful argument for the traditional history syllabus in secondary schools—in content if not in method—and it is to be hoped that the pressures for the project approach at this level will not reduce the status of mainstream history to that of an academic study. But this is a problem from which teachers of juniors are mercifully protected. Young children have no data bank against which to register what they hear about the world. In this respect, their position is similar to that of the peasantry before, say, mid-Victorian times (and indeed, as reminiscences of the time show, of a large sector of the population in 1914). To the people of rural England, war and rumours of war came with the inexplicability of a sudden thunderstorm. Troops were needed, in the same way as a force of labourers might be needed to rescue a damaged harvest. Many were called, and many were chosen. And off they went to war, knowing nothing about the cause for which they were fighting, caught inextricably in a web not of their own spinning.

Thus, today, children see on television films about wars in faraway places, and about civil disturbance nearer at hand. They have no means of knowing why there is guerilla warfare in south-east Asia, tension in the Middle East, or strife in Ulster. Sometimes, events may brush them more closely, as in 1939 when thousands of city children found themselves uprooted—for reasons which belonged exclusively to the adult world—from their familiar streets and transplanted to an alien countryside. We delude ourselves if we think that the contemporary world looks the same, viewed from childhood, as it does seen from our lofty vantage-point—or that the only thing needed to make it look the same is *information*. Small wonder that, however belligerent they may be in the playground, young children are pacifists at heart when it comes to national and international affairs.

The tradition of teaching young children about early civilisations is based partly on the concept of the child as a noble savage, confronting the same problems about the universe as did primitive man. If we start to examine what makes up the daily life of a contemporary child, this thesis immediately breaks down. Apart from the absence in primitive civilisations of Mister Softee ice-cream, Rice Krispies, sherbet dabs, *Dandy* and *Beano,* morning assembly, the new maths (or the old, for that matter), *Jackanory* and *Blue Peter,* the pattern of modern family life, even at the lowest levels, normally solves for children the main problem that primitive man had to face—how to survive.

What society *is* busy doing with children, both before we see them in school and afterwards through us as teachers, is—to borrow a phrase from Dr Desmond Morris—equipping them for the super-tribal world outside childhood. This is a process which, according to Dr Morris, begins immediately after birth. 'During the early months of its life,' he has written, 'a human baby passes through a sensitive socialisation phase when it develops a profound and long-lasting attachment to its species and especially to its mother.'[1] As the child grows older, it perceives

[1] *The Human Zoo,* by Desmond Morris. (Jonathan Cape, 1969.)

broadening sets of relationships: within its family unit (and including pets, the home and furniture as well as parents and siblings), within the social circle in which the family moves, within the street, the town, and so on. By the time we see children in school, their perception of relationships is still pretty simple, and still blurred at the edges.

Particularly with less able children, this simplicity and blurring persist well into the junior school age-range. It is common, for example, to find children of up to eight (and by no means rarely up to ten or so) describing almost any other child of roughly the same age as a 'cousin', while almost any adult female friend of the family is apt to be seen as an 'aunt'. Since many children are taught this usage of 'aunt', this is in some cases perhaps not significant, but the wide use of 'cousin' is derived not from usage, but from perception. All this illustrates how very limited a child's perception of the world is, and how impossible are the demands we make of him if we project him back two or three or even ten thousand years and expect him to accept figures from those periods as real people like himself, his brothers and sisters, and his 'cousins' and 'aunts'.

But with young children—say at the lower junior level—history cannot even start with their own families. It must start with themselves. In this way, the beginnings of history—or, to use a term more appropriate to the scale of the work, 'time studies'—link conveniently with the sort of 'news'-gathering which goes on naturally in most classrooms. As every teacher of primary children knows, objectives must be limited; it is not yet time to think in terms of giving children a sense of historical perspective, even in relation to their own history, but we can reasonably hope to get them to acknowledge that it exists—that there *is* such a concept as 'last year', and that 'last year' had a flavour recognisably different from this year's. A useful starting-point for a discussion with this aim is the subject of ages. To a child, his age is almost a personal possession, but the concept of age tends not to extend beyond precise knowledge of his own. Many children, for example, cannot easily see that a brother who is now, say, twelve can ever have been anything else. And as for the age of adults, accurate methods of estimating break down completely. Once, when I was talking about this with a class of eight-year-olds, I asked for estimates of my age. One tactless but confident boy estimated 63. As I was 27 at the time, I asked how he had arrived at this figure. 'I've counted you,' he replied. I never did find out what he meant, but there was no doubt that he had hit upon a method of calculating which satisfied him and which he was quite sure was accurate.

Most schools have enough of a traditional calendar to provide useful leads in this kind of discussion. Can the children remember last year's nativity play? (Yes, Nigel was nearly sick on stage, and Mrs Jones just managed to rush him off in time.) Last year's sports day? (Yes, we had orangeade that tasted of soapflakes.) Their last teacher? (Yes, she used to shout at you and her nose got all red.) When they were in the infants' school? The first day they came to school?

Invariably, children *can* remember this kind of thing—extremely well and in vivid detail. They remember not so much the sports day winners, but the taste of the orangeade; not what the nativity play was about, but Nigel nearly being sick in the manger. The collection of anecdotes that follows are from a batch I collected on tape from a group of ten-year-olds in a Somerset school. As stories they are, of course, trivial. But they illustrate—and they were all spoken impromptu into the tape-recorder—how powerfully the children's own past remains with them. It is important to remember, too, that as these stories were all collected from children in one class, some of them, or parts of them, were part of the common school experience of that particular group. Thus, inconsequential though the stories are in themselves, they are part of the history, and perhaps already becoming part of the folklore, of a tiny segment of Somerset society.

Judy: 'When I first went to school I was going home for dinner and I went up for Ronald and he wasn't there. So I went up my granny's to see if he was up there, but he went without me, so I didn't have no dinner that day.'

Linda: 'When I was eight years old I was in Mrs Cox's class. She was very nice then. One day I was going back in my writing, so she said "Linda, I wish you did pull your socks up." And I started pulling my socks up. And she said "No dear, that isn't the way to pull your socks up. I mean in your writing."'

David: 'I was five years old when I went to school and that day I didn't like it, but eventually I got used to it. One day we had a puppet show and Mrs Smith said "All of you must bring a puppet." My puppet's name was Hank, a cowboy on TV.'

Carol: 'Once when I was in Mrs Cox's class we had PE and I went down to get the hoops. And on the floor there was a kettle. I went and kicked the kettle over and all the water went out on the mat and there was a big stain on there. Mrs Cox went and took me to Mrs Jones, and she said "Tell her what you've done." But I wouldn't tell her so *she* told *me*. And they went and put the mat out and the chair out in the playground to dry.'

Children are always surprised to find that the trivia of their lives can possibly be of interest to anyone else. When I first started to record children's reminiscences of earlier schooldays—and even more noticeably later, when we moved on to skipping and counting rhymes and I urged them to take me outside and demonstrate some of these in action—they regarded me with profound suspicion; the more so because all this was taking place in periods clearly labelled on the timetable *English* or *History*. Soon, however, they began to sense—though not, of course, to define—

the point of my interest. I was demonstrating to them, *from* them, the outlines of their common culture.

It is salutary to remember that when children reminisce like this they are talking about a time as remote from their present selves as our early schooldays are from us—not in time, but in concept. To get children talking about their early childhood is to take them back into history as surely as (and I would say much more meaningfully than) taking them to see Stonehenge. There are all sorts of fascinating developments to be made from such a simple topic as, for example, 'Where did you first go to school?'. I once taught in a commuter village in Kent which had recently been developed by the building of several large housing estates. The people who came to live there were largely from south-east London. Typically, they were families who had just had their *second* child, so the older children tended to have been born and to have gone to their first school before the move. Plotting these first schools (or the children's birthplaces) on a large-scale map, and joining these places with pins and wool to the village where we all now lived showed up quite clearly an apparent mass migration. But this would have been a profitless and frustrating exercise in the Somerset school I mentioned earlier, because the family that had ever lived anywhere else but in that small town was an exception. On the other hand, the Somerset children compensated by the stability of their early lives. Thus, when they talked about their first days at school, we all knew the teachers and the classrooms they were talking about, and the teachers who had since retired or moved away were figures in history—their particular history—as surely as Boadicea or Richard II.

The span of the children's school lives is short enough, and packed with incident enough, to justify the use of a time-chart, perhaps as a group or class affair to which each child contributes. This should be largely pictorial, with perhaps a few examples of writing—creative or pure reminiscence—inserted at appropriate points. It is important to take the advice of the children on what should appear on the chart; it is, after all, about *their* lives, and, as I have already indicated, children and adults differ on their assessments of significance. Some quite trivial incident may seem just as important to a group of children as, say, one of the major events in the school year, and it is right to follow the children's lead in this. (Who can say which of the events of the past twenty years will be chosen to help make up the pattern of twentieth-century history?)

From the immediate history of the class and its members, it is an easy step to the history of their families. Perhaps the school is old enough, and the district stable enough in population, for some of the children's parents or even grandparents to have attended it. What was it like then? What were the teachers like? The school log book can often yield some interesting material here, particularly about the effect of national events upon the lives of teachers and children.

Here are a few examples of log book entries from Dringhouses School, York, which illustrate the potentialities of this particular form of archive.

December 17, 1915 : School closed this morning. The premises are being taken over by the Military Authorities for accommodation of troops.

May 3, 1916 : Owing to the Air Raid which kept most of the children out of bed until morning there were many absentees from school today.

November 3, 1916 : Some children have been excused in order to help farmers to get potatoes in.

May 6, 1921 : Early in Spring the garden class pruned the lower branches of the plane trees alongside the banking facing the school. Owing to the Miners' Strike the branches have been sawn into logs and used on the School fires.

March 2, 1923 : This morning, the wind being contrary, the fire in the stove had to be raked out, as the downdraught filled the room with sulphur fumes.

December 16, 1929 : The Airship R100 (the largest in the world) was launched at Howden near Hull this morning and passed very close to the school at 9 a.m. It was seen by all the scholars in brilliant early sunshine after a frosty morning.

September 30, 1938 : On Wednesday, owing to the national emergency, the scholars were measured for respirators and in the evening adults were also measured. On Thursday 4.15 the Secretary for Education (G. H. Gray Esq.) and the Clerk of Works visited the school premises to decide upon a suitable site for Air Raid Shelters.

March 12, 1941 : No morning school as the All Clear did not sound until 3.45 p.m.

May 4, 1945 : At 11 a.m. a 'Welcome Home' Celebration was held in the school in honour of old boys Walter Doughty and Frank Heald . . . both prisoners of war for some years in Germany . . . over fifty parents were present . . . this was one of the most moving ceremonies ever held in this school.[2]

Entries like these—taken almost at random from the log book of a very ordinary school—can be the starting-points for a whole series of history inquiries. There will be grandparents who can remember the night of the Zeppelin raid, parents who can remember the homecoming the school gave to Walter Doughty and Frank Heald; and so on. At once, history has leapt out of books to become something that happened to someone the children know.

This, of course, is only a beginning. School photographs, and perhaps

[2] *The History of Dringhouses School, 1863–1970,* by R. C. Stott. (Dringhouses Primary School, York, PTA, 1970.)

clippings from local newspapers kept in the school archives, can be equally useful, and prompted by this cue (and by the excitement of exploring unplumbed cupboards) the children can be encouraged to bring similar souvenirs from home. (Always take great care of photographs and other offerings from home, of course. They are doubtless irreplaceable, and failure to return them in the same condition as they were lent is unforgiveable, and will remain unforgiven!)

We are now beginning to amass a variety of sources which can form the basis for a number of different topics. The school itself and the material which should be readily available about it could absorb one or more groups for many weeks. Another group (perhaps chosen with some care, and I shall be looking more closely at this question later) could be set to work to construct family trees. A third could examine the growth of the district, breaking down development into fairly easy stages such as: before the First World War, between the wars, post-war.

Here, however, some words of warning are appropriate. No one who has followed the kind of story about education that gets big coverage in the popular papers (*Teacher in family quiz row*), and indeed no teacher with an ordinary amount of sensitivity, needs to be told that any classroom topic which touches upon the children's homes and families needs to be handled with care. There are teachers who, in the interests of some environmental project or even to provide a bank of statistics for use in maths, have sent their pupils home with what amounted to duplicated census forms, only to be surprised when parents sent the forms back to school (or, even worse, to the education officer) with pithy instructions on what to do with them. None of my readers would be foolish enough to let themselves in for that, if only because the mass gathering of information is not the object of this particular exercise, but before we consider further the possibilities of history through family affairs it is perhaps worth making a few points of warning and advice.

However delicately the teacher may tread, it is not unlikely that a junior child will go home to report that his teacher was asking who his grandfather was and what he did. This sort of thing can cause endless difficulty—often, oddly enough, with parents who have least reason to be sensitive on the subject. In many schools, though, trouble can be avoided by telling parents what your plans are. If there is a thriving parent-teacher association, you could take ten minutes or so at one of its meetings to explain what you are about. Or you could send home a duplicated letter with the same objective.

In either case, avoid the approach: 'Don't be surprised if your child comes home and asks you your mother's maiden name, because we're going to do a project on family trees.' Remember that in the end the success of a project based on family life will depend upon the goodwill of parents in providing exhibits and information. Your introductory letter could go something like this:

Dear Parent,

Young children learning history often have great difficulty in understanding time. If you have only been living for eight years, the idea of 'twenty years ago' or 'a thousand years ago' is hard to grasp. Because of this, I'm going to let the children in Class X do some work about recent history, so that instead of having to think about 'twenty years ago' they can think about 'when my Dad was a boy'—an idea which they can grasp much more easily.

So we're going to do some work about what life was like when you were young. I'm letting you know about this because your child might, in the next few weeks, come home with some strange requests—including requests for the loan of old family photographs, or for stories about your childhood. Anything you lend us for this project will, of course, be looked after very carefully.

I hope you'll be able to help, because if you can you'll be helping all of us to find out what history means.

This should have the effect of defusing any possible bombshells that could result from your project. But if you feel that it is impossible to get the parents of your class on your side, you can still explore history in this particular way without putting the project on such a personal level. Of course, by sparking off the inquiries through the school log book and what parents can remember of the events noted in it, you may well unleash such a flood of reminiscence that no possible difficulty (except perhaps the question of when and how to stem the tide) should occur.

I have assumed so far that whatever work is done will be organised on some kind of group or individual or pair basis. It is important, though, that each study should not remain in isolation for ever—and the younger the children involved, the more important it is. The objectives of history teaching at this age are still fairly broad, and they tend to boil down to answers to the question: what was it *like* then? All the topics should therefore be brought together at the end so that children can make their own cross-references from school to family, from family to district, and so on. It is pointless for a child to have an intimate knowledge of the history of the school, say, without being able to relate it to his own family, without being able to say, of an event that took place in 1939, how old his mother and father were then, what was happening to them, and what his home district was like at that time. At the end of a series of group projects, some linking device is therefore needed to weld the separate parts together into a comprehensible whole.

There are a number of ways of doing this. The traditional way might be a pageant, but this particular dramatic form is perhaps *too* traditional for modern teachers. A less mannered form of drama, however, makes an effective way of bringing the threads of group work together. With a rather older group of children than the lower juniors we are at present thinking about, I once organised a dramatic history of a local railway line—the Somerset and Dorset, which was at that time about to close to passenger traffic. In this, we spanned about 130 years, and the wider historical horizons of eleven-year-olds enabled us to take in some fragments of Victorian history, the development of new local industries and the parallel decline of the old ones, changes in fashion, changes in the style of family outings, and even a number of family histories since members of some of the children's families had worked on the line. During the 1970 celebrations of the centenary of state education, I saw another effective dramatic round-up of local history at a school where it was decided to hold an ingenious 'open day' in which each class represented a different generation. The result was a sort of living museum of education, and of manners, costume and other exhibits, reminiscent in style of the Geffrye Museum in London.

Displays of original sources and other exhibits are also useful in giving the work a focal point. I have already mentioned school and family souvenirs in this connection. Other useful items include examples of handcrafts, parents' old exercise books (it's surprising how many of these are kept in attics!), old toys (also often faithfully kept), and newspaper cuttings about the school and the district. In some areas, the school museum service can often help, particularly with small items of craftwork.

With older children, an historical background to the more local items can often be sketched in with the judicious use of items from the excellent reproductions of first-hand source material available in Evans' *History at Source* series, Jonathan Cape's *Jackdaws,* and similar archive publications. (More detailed notes on these valuable aids are given in the source list.) With young children, however, it is important, I think, to confine the centre of interest to their *own* lives and immediate families'. History must be well-rooted in their own community, and the community which, for young children, is really their own is a very narrow one. Thus I would tend to exclude, unless the area is a coal-mining one where memories are long, such pieces of social history as the scandal of child labour in the mines; and I would exclude also, unless I were teaching in, say, Bath or Cheltenham, items concerned with high fashion and the pastimes of the rich. For lower juniors, immediate relevance to the children is the main criterion in determining the scope of a class's inquiries into the past, and however fascinating some of the by-ways of possible research may be to the teacher, the temptation to stray beyond the limitations imposed by the children should be firmly resisted.

There are, of course, exceptions. An example of how an unexpected and apparently alien source can spark off interest comes, again, from my teaching in Somerset. Again with a class of older juniors, we were pursuing the topic of surnames, of which this particular town had a fine and unusual crop; we had also touched on the fact that many of the children's families had lived in the town for generations. Not very much of great importance happens in small Somerset towns, but something of less than usual tranquillity had happened in this one some 120 years before, when about twenty miners had been killed in the crash of a pit cage. The event was recorded on a much-weathered, but just decipherable, tombstone in the churchyard, together with, unusually and I believe uniquely for a tombstone, the accusation that the rope whose failure had sent the twenty miners crashing to their deaths had been deliberately cut. Though of antiquarian interest, this discovery would have been beyond the scope of our project on surnames had it not been for the inscription among the names on the stone of the names of what must have been the forebears of a sizeable proportion of the class. It was a link with the past too clear-cut to be ignored.

Generally, however, such things are luxuries. Our prime effort in teaching history with juniors must be to get across the idea of *sequence* over whatever period we are studying, and this is where activities of the type I described earlier—the history of the railway line and the historical open day—are so valuable. Everyone who deals with children knows that they see time past—time, that is, before they were born—in a kind of distorting-mirror. This accounts for those gasp-making occasions when children ask if one remembers the first cars, or the first trains, or the last dinosaurs. Children are now the recipients, through television, of so much ill-assorted information (they may see an historical play at five o'clock, and an episode of a science-fiction story set in AD 3000 at six) that their confusion is doubly confounded. There were many schools in which projects based on the first American moon landing went off at half-cock because many children did not realise that a landing had not already been achieved years before. If we can give children, in the junior school, a framework by which to measure time that they have not actually experienced at first hand, we shall have provided them with an essential tool for living as well as with the basic equipment for further historical study.

Chapter 3

Finding sources

Although it is important that history in the junior school should be rooted in the children's own experience, through their personal and families' lives, this is not to say that it should stay there for good. In any case, of course, group or individual work has a way of using up material at a frightening rate, and the scope of study must be broadened if only to help to sustain the syllabus.

In practice, the cue for historical work to take a less parochial turn will often come spontaneously, either from the children themselves or from the demands of an integrated timetable. During the project on the local railway line which I mentioned in the last chapter, a boy brought along a book of his father's, dated in the early 1930s, with some such title as *The Boy's Book of Steam Locomotives*. His group went to work merrily with this, and before long their local line had been lost sight of in the study of such more attractive topics as the American transcontinental railways with their big, powerful, head-lamped, 'cow-catcher' locomotives. Soon, they were investigating the opening up of the American Middle West; a far cry from the simple, homely affairs of the Somerset and Dorset Joint Railway. It did not seem easy (or particularly important) to devise a means of bringing this wayward group back on to the rails I had chosen for their study, and in fact I never tried.

Generally, however, the teacher's problem is not to stem, or try to control, the flow of interest but to keep it going without literally putting everything into the children's hands. Whatever educational idealists may say, in real classrooms children just *don't* get so fired with enthusiasm, whether about new maths or history or creative writing or anything else, that they romp away with nothing more from the teacher to help them on their way than an encouraging wave. The teacher has to be fairly adept at injecting new ideas and new sources at the appropriate time. At the same time, if the kind of history curriculum I am advocating in this book is to have any advantage at all over the traditional race from Stonehenge to Stephenson, the teacher must not organise his expectations too rigidly.

There is quite a dilemma here, and it is one common to all modern teaching methods. The cynical observer watching a class progress through modern maths, for example, by discovery and experience may well wonder at the unfailing inevitability with which a group, having 'discovered' the principle of sets, goes on to 'discover' intersecting sets, which prove (surprise, surprise) to be on the next page of the teacher's book. Why is it, it may be asked, that a group making sets of domestic animals never gets sidetracked at this point into the study of different breeds of dogs, say, in a project that occupies them for weeks and may indeed take in a lot of useful maths, but which never advances them along the narrow path that leads to the next mathematical topic ordained by the Nuffield Foundation? When the children's interests quarrel with the teacher's, who, even in an age of child-centred education, wins?

Fortunately, the objectives in history teaching are less clearly defined, but, all the same, the teacher has to guard against filling the void with some of his own. He must also guard against the temptation to make his teaching merely a vehicle for his own interests; and the more he is interested in his subject, the more difficult this becomes.

It seems to me that perhaps the best role the teacher can play is that of 'nudger'. He must have some idea of the way things *can* go, rather than the way he *wants* them to go, and he must be equipped to suggest a new line of inquiry, to produce some new, interesting piece of source material, and to lead the children subtly and gradually outward from 'first person' history to local, regional and national topics. At the same time, it is a mistake to stray away too soon from personal topics, though the temptation to make, as it were, for the historical shore, where one can bask in the comfort and luxury of ample, easily obtainable references, is often almost overpowering.

The kinds of activities described in the last chapter should have given the children some kind of yardstick by which to measure time past; not yet a complete and infallible instrument, of course, but something to be going along with. One of the regular features of history teaching in the junior school, if it is to become anything more than a series of disjointed anecdotes and 'points of interest', must be constant cross-referencing—almost a kind of 'time drill' to ensure that children are building up, through their projects, concepts of sequence and contemporaneity. This applies equally to older-established approaches as to the one I am describing. The weakness of so many recent approaches to junior school history over the past two or three decades has been their failure to achieve this important linking of topics. In their anxiety to break away from lists of dates, battles and monarchs, the innovators have expelled from the syllabus the one link that makes history comprehensible. (It is worth noting, in passing, that junior geography teaching is prone to the same trap. It is all too easy to gallop through a sequence of studies of different parts of the world without doing anything like enough work with an atlas for it to become clear how these snippets of world life stand in relation to one another.)

Children who have been subjected to 'patch' history—the in-depth study, from a variety of angles, of a small segment of time—may, as a result of enlightened and skilled teaching, have a good knowledge of events in the various 'patches' which they have studied, but all too often fail to find out how one 'patch' relates to another. This kind of failure is, of course, not confined to this particular method, nor to the junior school. With syllabuses based on the periods dictated by O-level examiners and their apparent conviction that the world periodically changed overnight during such years as 1485 and 1789, whoever bothers about what was going on in 1484 or 1788?

Similarly, children who have worked through one project topic after another—transport, communications, discovery and exploration, domestic furniture, clothing and costume, and so on—often fail to see each topic in its context. When this happens, it reduces history to the level of a cigarette-card collection.

The most readily available setting against which the disparate parts of early historical knowledge can be placed remains the local community. Before I go into this further, I have to declare implacable war on a fashion which grew up in the 1950s of raking over the dry husks of antiquarian records in search of classroom material. During this period, student teachers had urged upon them the value in teaching terms (and even junior school teaching terms) of such archives as manorial Court Rolls, Select Vestry Minutes, excerpts from Domesday Book and similar antiquarian hunting-grounds. This, it seems to me, is another example of the way in which the academic historian falls down badly in his judgement of suitable material for him to use as a teacher. Just as in the first chapter of this book we had John Fines urging teachers to tell dissident teenagers about Marius and Sulla, we have seen over the past fifteen years or so advisers like John West[1] recommending six-week studies of Court Rolls which—and I find this impossible to believe, but it is John West's claim—'resulted in an authentic imaginative response which was more than merely imitative of the records'. This is rather like claiming that an imaginative account of contemporary life could be reasonably based on a study of council minutes and general rate demands.

[1] *History here and now*, by John West. (Schoolmaster, 1966.)

The immediate stimulus of this approach was the development of electrostatic copying, which made available for the first time comparatively cheap prints of archive material. But in school it found a ready response, I suspect, because of the inbuilt antiquarian leanings of many teachers. The class visit to the local church has long been one of the annual rituals in many schools; the sudden availability of records rooted in the same building must have seemed to many teachers almost too good to be true.

For a savage analysis of the dangers and follies of antiquarianism, aptly illustrating the perils on whose brink we stand when we teach local history, I recommend John Betjeman's essay on *Antiquarian prejudice*, written in 1937 but no less appropriate today. Betjeman points out how two writers on a fictitious village—the author of a formal local guide and a more prosy *Highways and Byways* man—are both obsessed with such trivia as the Early English piscina in the north porch of the church (left there, as Betjeman points out, by a forgetful and confused church restorer) and say nothing about what the village is really like. 'The church is the one building in the village of no interest at all,' writes Betjeman, yet it is the only building referred to in either of his quotations. The only objects of interest are the people: 'but antiquarianism is not interested in people.'[2]

Dogged pursuit of the history curriculum in local churches still persists, however, and in the most surprising places. I know the head of what is in some ways a very progressive school who still bases much of his history teaching, as well as a good deal of art and craft work, on churches, and who even pursues the same theme when he takes a school party each summer into the country for a week. His school is in the centre of a city, where perhaps one needs least of all to look to churches as a focal point for local history; the venue of the annual school journey is mid-Dorset, where there is a range of historical study topics to suit all tastes—from the barrows and crop-marks of prehistory, through the once thriving but now dead woollen industry to the recent closures of local railway lines. I find it sad that, surrounded as these children are by the real stuff of history, they are apparently condemned for ever to studies of church buildings and relics.

History is, in fact, about people, and people are closest, outside their families, to their work. The leading industries of an area make a good starting-point for investigation of local history. Often, the larger local firms have useful records which they are prepared to make available, or copies of company histories which can be borrowed. Some even keep up a small museum of exhibits relating to their early days to which they will admit visiting parties. Sometimes, older employees have valuable memories of their early working lives which cast an interesting light on earlier working conditions and standards of living.

The growth of interest, in recent years, in what is known rather

[2] *First and last loves*, by John Betjeman. (John Murray, 1952.)

unattractively as industrial archaeology has been a boon to teachers wishing to draw for teaching material on local industrial sources. It is true that industrial archaeology has its academics, over-keen to enthuse too readily over minor modifications of, say, Victorian steam-hammers, but the effect of the boom in industrial archaeology has been to release for general use a vast amount of archive material which had lain hidden for years and may well, had it not been for the enthusiasts, have been lost for ever.

How rich the new sources are varies enormously, of course, from area to area according to the degree of activity of local enthusiasts. Generally, areas within the hinterland of a university, particularly one of the newer universities, are fortunate. There are one or two other pockets where the activity of industrial archaeologists has been intense, sometimes under the guidance of local authorities. In other places, the teacher may have to fend for himself.

Some examples will, perhaps, be useful. Teachers who work in or near Swindon are particularly fortunate, because this was the town chosen by a former BBC West Region industrial correspondent, Kenneth Hudson, for detailed study in a book which has since become a model of its type.[3] Since then, the formerly strong railway influence on the town has been reflected in its choice as the site of one of Britain's major museums of railway relics, given over largely to the development of the Great Western Railway and to the careers of its two creators, Brunel and Gooch. Added to this, the development of a stretch of Wiltshire downland (for, until the middle of the nineteenth century, Swindon was a small market town a mile away from the present centre, in the area now known as Old Town) into a Victorian industrial complex can still clearly be traced from existing buildings. Even one of the major churches in Swindon was created by the railway. With the railway museum on his doorstep, ample source material available in any standard history of the British railway system, excellent opportunities for field work, an excellent local public library well aware of what made Swindon tick, and even a readily-available account[4] of what working life was like before the First World War, teachers in Swindon are particularly well supplied with sources for local history studies. (Here, incidentally, is an example of how irrelevant Court Rolls and Domesday Book and even the *Victoria County History* can be for our purpose. Everything with any bearing at all on contemporary life in Swindon has happened since 1830 or so.)

Few areas are as fortunate as this, however. In most places, sources of material have to be dug for, though the situation is improving as industrial archaeology groups work further and further afield. The handful of coal-mines in the Midsomer Norton/Radstock area of Somerset which are all that is left of the Somerset coalfield offer extensive help

[3] *An awkward size for a town,* by Kenneth Hudson. (David and Charles, 1967.)
[4] *Life in a railway factory,* by Alfred Williams. (David and Charles, 1969.)

to teachers in that area. Even recent Ordnance Survey maps reveal how extensive, until very recently, the coalfield was; there is an excellent first-hand account of life in one of the pit villages in the late eighteenth and early nineteenth centuries from its parson; the industrial archaeology unit of Bristol City Museum has done some useful research; and, of course, there is plenty of material evidence in the two towns that dependence on mining was their main driving-force until about fifteen years ago. A few miles away is the village of Mells, the former home of Fussell's, a notable firm of agricultural implement manufacturers. In 1965, a substantial part of Fussell's foundry was still standing, though derelict, and this both cast an interesting light on the past of an area now entirely agricultural and reflected the industrial past—largely unsuspected by those who know Somerset only in its more picturesque aspects—of the area still in abundant evidence only a few miles distant.

The invention of the tape-recorder, and in particular the development of comparatively cheap reliable portable machines, has added another dimension to local history studies. Although the *bona fides* of 'oral history' have yet to be accepted by academic historians, there is no doubt that it affords immense scope in school. Interviewing is, of course, a skill which calls for training, and the collection of taped interviews from local people can come only after much preparatory activity, and probably only with children who, from years of practice, have become thoroughly familiar with the use of the tape-recorder. It should be said here that this work is only worth attempting if the children do it. It is surprising how efficiently children can use relatively complex machinery, in fact, and many a ham-fisted teacher using recorders, film-projectors and the like in school has been saved from disaster by the know-how of upper juniors.

For outside work, recording speech, a light portable cassette machine —the standard cassette Philips, for example—should be used. Provided the basic rules about acoustics are observed, this should produce quite adequate results. As cassettes are relatively expensive and also extremely difficult to edit, however, recordings from them should be transferred to ordinary tape, using a larger machine of the type most schools have. Few children are capable of producing recordings sufficiently polished to be worth retaining complete, but on the other hand most interviews will yield something worth preserving.

Help with the techniques of transferring recordings from one tape to another, and of editing, can be obtained from one of any number of handbooks on amateur tape-recording, and D. Neville Wood's *On Tape* (Ward Lock Educational, 1970) is also useful.

The diversity of the work which can be done once the archive of oral history is unlocked by the tape-recorder is considerable. Here is a quotation from a taped interview with a 69-year-old resident of Whitstable, Kent, who was recalling her childhood in the East End of

London. This interview was, in fact, the first to be collected by Kent University for its archive of oral history, to which many schools have since contributed.

'My father used to take me down through the Bethnal Green Road and I remember it very vividly. . . We would pass the pubs which were all open and the women would take their vegetables and sit in the pub. They used to wear coarse aprons which was a piece of sacking and they had a cap on their heads, probably their husbands' you know, and they'd sit in the pubs.

'I suppose it must have been summer because the doors were all open. They'd sit in these bars and do their peas and beans and anything they could in the way of vegetables and previously they'd sent their children to the baker's to cook the Sunday joint and while that was being cooked the children used to play outside, and that was the usual Sunday practice of the people in the East End.'[5]

This picture of Sunday in the East End is in marked contrast to the impression of Sunday piety which we are often given in recollections of turn-of-the-century life by middle-class writers. There was, however, plenty of piety about, as is shown in this recollection of life at about the same time in a Kentish village now swallowed up by suburban development.

'There used to be temperance rallies at Dartford, and we used to walk over sometimes, or we'd go over on one of the farm carts. And on the way back—it'd be getting dark—we used to sing the old temperance songs, like:

> Shut up your public houses!
> Shut up your public houses!
> Shut up your public houses!
> We don't want none of your beer!
> We don't want none of your beer!
> We're all teetotallers here!
> Shut up your public houses!
> . . . and so on.

'We were all Baptists in our family, and I remember my mother was walking past the village hall one day with the Baptist minister's wife. As they went past, there was some kind of meeting going on inside, and they were all singing a music-hall song. And the minister's wife turned to my mother and said in a shocked tone of voice: "I don't like the sound of that, Mrs ———, do you?" '

[5] *Oral history and its possibilities in schools,* by John Wyman. Kent Education Gazette, Vol. LII, No. 1.

It would come as a shock to the children of this present-day community of middle-class suburbanites to find how feudal the village—
only about fifteen miles from central London—was even quite late in
living memory. Similarly, it is salutary to remember that the living
conditions of ordinary people were until quite recently intolerable by
today's standards. Here is the Whitstable woman again, remembering her
East End home in the early years of this century:

> 'There was very little comfort. The décor, if one could call it
> such in those days, as I look back, it was shocking. It was stained
> oak varnished paper, and one never had any change all the years
> that I can remember as a child. The wallpaper was the same. It
> was religiously washed down every so often, but it was always this
> awful brown. The woodwork was stained and varnished. Everything
> was stained brown and varnished. . . It was considered good
> enough. Everything was drab. Everything was dingy.'

Working procedures as well as details of domestic and social life are
effectively recalled in interviews. Here is a former boatman on the
Bridgwater Canal in Lancashire recalling how he and his workmates
used to 'leg' their narrow boats through the tunnels while the horses
walked over the hill to pick up the boats again at the other end:

> 'A happy lot we were, master. Yes, happy, that we were!
> Legging? Well, we just took it as it come. We put the boards out
> on each side of the boat, at the front, and fastened them there.
> Then we slipped a half-sack of corn under us as a cushion, see,
> and just walked our way along the sides of the tunnel . . . weaving
> our feet over each other, lying half-sideways all the time. We just
> kept on walking! It took us about two hours and a half, master,
> and very damp it was, too. Dripping damp, and dark. Of course,
> we did have a wick lighted, sometimes two. And when we got
> back to Middlewich, well, I've seen fifteen or maybe twenty boats
> lined up outside the King's Head and a melodeon soon got going
> and nobody thought any more about locks and legging!'[6]

It would be over-optimistic to suppose that many juniors will be able
to call forth reminiscences of this evocative power, but it must be
remembered at the same time that these are doubtless the highlights
from interviews which may have taken several hours or even days to
record. But what these quotations do indicate is how much useful
material is ignored unless we take steps to bring children into contact
with first-hand reminiscence. Often, too, the insights given in this way
are not commonly found in print; there are plenty of photographs of
life in the East End of London at the turn of the century, but how

[6] *Canals and waterways,* by A. H. Body. (University of London Press, 1969.)

many people remember now that the cooking of Sunday joints was a regular part of a baker's work? (Incidentally, the practice of taking joints along to the baker persisted up to recent times in some areas, particularly at Christmas-time when large family gatherings involved cooking beyond the resources of the family oven. Now that there are few 'behind the shop' bakers, it must have died out, which is a pity since modern domestic cookers are even less able than old-fashioned ones to cope with big roasts.)

There is a limited amount of first-hand reminiscence available on records, as will be noted in the list of sources later, but it is unfortunate that much valuable material is virtually locked away, and out of reach so far as the teacher is concerned, in such places as the sound libraries of the British Institute of Recorded Sound, the English Folk Dance and Song Society and the BBC Sound Archives.[7] It is to be hoped that at some time a record manufacturer will get around to producing a recorded equivalent of *Jackdaws,* using this fund of raw material and making it available for general use. Meanwhile, we have to do the best we can; perhaps by recording, perhaps by inviting old people to come along and talk about their young days, perhaps by taking groups of children to visit them. There are also a few printed accounts available which can be used with discretion, and these too are mentioned in the source list.

All this source material—from the printed word, from recordings, from field work, from family stories—must, if it is to have teaching value, be used to create a new form of the children's own, whether this is through art and craft, creative writing, drama, or whatever. A group could, for example, create its own 'reminiscences' on tape of the working and domestic life of their neighbourhood, based on their own research. This can often be very effective, especially if combined with folksong and some of the other aspects of traditional culture to which I refer in a later chapter. This kind of work cannot, however, be started 'cold', and a good way to get children thinking in terms of giving an impression of a way of life is to get them to write or record what life is like for them, today, on the assumption that their work is to be stored away to give children living in a hundred years' time some idea of life now. One of the great values of a 'dummy run' project of this kind is that it readily shows up the sort of things (taking the joint to the baker, for example) which cannot easily be found out from other sources. In its own right, of course, as a medium for a variety of forms of expression, a 'history of our time' project has immense value.

[7] The sound libraries of the BIRS and the EFDSS are, however, open to the public and operate a free listening service which teachers may use, though it is not possible either to borrow material or transcribe it. School parties are not admitted to these libraries. The address of the British Institute of Recorded Sound is: 29 Exhibition Road, London SW7; and of the English Folk Dance and Song Society: Cecil Sharp House, 2 Regents Park Road, London NW1. Preliminary inquiries are essential in both cases.

At best a class can, so to speak, pay in to the historical bank as well as draw from it. An excellent example of this comes from the Warwickshire village of Dunnington, where children aged seven to eleven in the village school carried out a number of village survey projects which were eventually lodged with the County Records Office. The surveys covered a wide variety of topics, including the way Dunnington children spent their time. (On average, seven minutes a day washing, except at the weekend when the time rose to fifteen minutes; thirty minutes a day helping their mothers during the week, forty minutes on Saturdays and Sundays.) Having made their contribution to future local history, the children went on to find out what Dunnington's past had to offer to them. As it turned out, there was plenty, and they recorded it with, as *The Times* reported, 'a good deal more truth than the local library might provide or the tourists gain when visiting Lord Hertford's house:

"A man could make a good life for himself and cheer his family up now and then at a hanging of a highwayman on the gibbet at Savage's Field where Hillers now grow such wonderful apples. But all this ended because a Prince of Wales wished to visit his friends the Hertfords at Ragley. To approach it the road from Evesham led over highwayman infested waste. The Prince was rather a coward and needed a quieter approach. So Dunnington Heath was enclosed by Act of Parliament." [8]

The phrase 'where Hillers now grow such wonderful apples' indicates that the Dunnington project was sparked off by a teacher who did not neglect to make links between past and present wherever possible.

Although there are many excellent books which provide background references for projects on recent history—and some of these are listed at the end of this book—there are still nothing like enough—and virtually none specifically geared to the junior school. So the teacher must find what he can for himself. Old newspapers and magazines, old sets of family encyclopaedias of the sort that turn up at school jumble sales, outdated local guidebooks and street directories, estate agents' old stocks of street plans all prove useful. Among contemporary periodicals, the colour supplements and country and county magazines often yield background information and illustrations relating to, respectively, social history (especially motoring and fashion) and local industries and customs. The 'Fifty Years Ago' columns of local newspapers are another source of information on local affairs.

The haphazard collection of bits and pieces of this sort can, of course, be a threat to the gainful employment of school time, and is worse than useless if not kept in some kind of order. Here is a chance for a group of children to learn the invaluable skills of indexing and cataloguing, starting with very broad, simple classifications like 'Fashions', 'Sports and pastimes', 'Railways' and so on. Two or three keen archivists in a class can make all the difference between desultory searching for

[8] *The Times*, 11 June 1971.

information through a cupboardful of historical junk and making exactly the same collection an invaluable part of the class's work. I would not personally go so far as to have a card-index catalogue of each item, though some teachers might feel that this is useful, but certainly there should be some kind of list of the material available. If a second-hand filing cabinet (often obtainable from government surplus stores) or map cabinet is available for the storage of items, so much the better; but a good deal of material can be safely stored in manila folders kept upright in cardboard boxes.

The habit of collecting odd pieces of reference material can sometimes lead to new lines of inquiry. An example of this occurred in one school from a newspaper cutting describing a sale of marine chronometers—vital instruments at sea before the introduction of wireless telegraphy, since the accuracy of navigation depended on working out latitude and longitude with the help of an absolutely spot-on chronometer. This led the children to consider how people on land managed for timekeeping when there were no BBC time signals. When they traced the pattern of their daily lives, their reliance on the BBC became obvious. How did the duty teacher know when to ring the bell? He went by his watch. How did he know his watch was right? He checked it every morning by the BBC pips. It was noted, in passing, that to some extent radio and television had taken the place of the clock in the home; a large clock on the living-room mantelpiece is no longer the dominant feature of a living-room that it once was. (Some grandparents' homes, though, it was reported, still had a clock, often a wedding present, in a place of honour.)

Then the class moved back in time to consider pre-BBC public timekeeping. 'Knockers-up' and factory hooters were discussed, and so was the prominence of large clocks on public buildings. The children were surprised to realise that only in recent times—since the creation of the railway system, in fact—did a national system of timekeeping become important. They found out how Greenwich Mean Time took over from 'local time' which had served well enough previously. They considered the prominence of clocks on village churches, and noted that, clocks being among the earliest examples of precision machinery and therefore expensive, these must often have been enormously costly in proportion to the rest of the fabric.

This illustrates, I think, a treatment of time as an historical topic which was more meaningful than the water clock—candle clock—sundial sequence usually studied in junior schools, not only because the latter is so speculative but also because the project I have described sprang from life *today*.

Both starting-points and reference material for projects can often be found in the most surprising places. One source that I have often found fruitful is the glossier kind of company brochure or house journal. Some years ago, the Unilever house journal printed a profusely-illustrated history of the company's soap advertising, starting with a W. G. Grace testimonial for Hudson's soap, and this led to an interesting study with upper juniors of advertising in general. The children were interested to find that the use of well-known personalities to sell the advertising message—familiar to them from television—was not new; an 1880 advertisement had a picture of Grace with the recommendation: 'Hudson's Soap for flannels.' A Sunlight Soap advertisement from 1907 was particularly interesting. It showed a traditional washerwoman with bonnet, apron, bowl and bucket, and it introduced the health angle. 'Sunlight Soap,' read the legend, 'saves the Clothes Bill, the Labour Bill and the Doctor's Bill.' By 1934, the health message had become more hysterical, and Unilever's advertising copywriters were now appealing to the people who actually *used* the soap rather than to those who just bought it for their servants to use: 'Are you quick to act against dirt dangers?' screamed the headline in an advertisement for Lifebuoy, above copy which was full of words like 'infection', 'antiseptic', 'germs' and so on. This particular advertisement ended with a 'medical scientist' declaring: 'Cleanliness is recognised today as one of the great forces in preventing the transfer of infection.' In more recent examples, information gave way to inducements. In 1953, Sunlight was offering Coronation seats or television sets in an 'easy-to-enter' competition. Two years later, 'brides' were being offered a sample pack of six free tablets of Puritan Soap and a thirty-two page booklet on home washing.

Another similar source of useful information which I came across while writing this chapter was the 1971 company report of the Army and Navy Stores, in which the centenary of the London department store was celebrated by a glossy, well-illustrated company history. This included photographs of the store's car showroom in 1928, fashions from various periods over the past hundred years, and a host of other valuable information including price lists which revealed not only the staggering increase in costs but also changes in buying habits.[9]

The possibilities of Ordnance Survey maps as historical documents should not be ignored—and it is not particularly important for this purpose that they should be up-to-date ones. It *is* important, though, not to introduce map work too soon, because this is a skill which young children find it hard to acquire. If any fieldwork is planned, however, along the lines to be described in the next chapter, the ability to use OS maps is invaluable, if not essential, and they are vital sources for tracing such footprints of recent history as the lines of old railways, the sites of abandoned airfields and so on. Mention must also be made at this point of the excellent series of reprints of first edition Ordnance Survey maps published by David and Charles. These are not easy sources for children to use, because they are printed in black only

[9] Probably the best pictorial guide to social life before the First World War is provided by the Army and Navy Stores Catalogue for 1907, published in facsimile by David and Charles.

and topography is shown by hachuring, but for those who are used to map work they provide almost complete local histories in themselves.

Maps only come to life, of course, if they are taken outside; and this is an appropriate point at which to turn to fieldwork, which can be the most rewarding aspect of junior and middle school history.

Chapter 4

Fieldwork

Inevitably, exposition rather than exploration must be the dominant element in historical fieldwork with children of school age, and the usual order of events in fieldwork is reversed. Children who are taken on a field trip must have a good idea of what they are expected to look for, and enough background knowledge to enable them to employ their observations effectively.

It should go without saying that historical fieldwork must be meticulously planned. The 'nature walk' approach, in which a class sets out 'to see what it can see', is entirely out of place here, and is, indeed, a passport to frustration, lack of interest, and maybe even disaster. Generally, a number of short trips with strictly limited objectives is preferable to a long one in which too much ground, both physically and historically, is covered.

Some of these objectives, particularly with younger children, can be very simple indeed: perhaps simply to take a look at a local building, or at the site of a Roman road, or at a tollhouse, or at a derelict railway line. But there will be scope even in such simple trips not only for imaginative work but also for that essential training in observation and recording which will prove so valuable later on. There should be no windmill or water-mill, no building of any age or significance, no abandoned industrial site, no relic of a recent, but now past, way of life in the area of the school that should not be visited provided that it is safe and legal to do so.

A word of warning here. Any field trip should be undertaken beforehand *without* the children. Not only will this enable the teacher to plan more accurately for the real thing, but it will also reveal problems of access or other difficulties which may not be obvious from printed or hearsay sources. I remember once taking a school party to Glastonbury Tor in Somerset. All the guide-books recommended an ascent from the north, over stiles which were clearly marked and following what was, to judge from the printed evidence, a well-defined route. And so, on arrival, it seemed to be; it was only when we started on our way that I discovered that the path led through a veritable swamp, crossed an almost impenetrable hedge, and then disappeared in the steep slope of the Tor itself. Some children, alarmed at the speed with which they were rising from the Sedgemoor plain, panicked and refused to go either forward or back. By this time, their shoes and socks were caked with mud, and we were all thoroughly miserable. We decided to skirt the edge of the Tor to see if there was a better way up from the other side; and so there proved to be—a gently rising causeway which, if I had done a preliminary trip of my own, I should have discovered.

The historical field trip is one occasion when the old-fashioned college discipline of thorough lesson preparation comes into its own. It really is no kind of teaching, and no kind of fun, to find yourself stranded with a class of children in the middle of a muddy, cowpat-riddled field with the girls whimpering with cold from their wet feet and the boys telling you what their mums will do with them when they get home with mudcaked shoes. Apart from these physical hazards, proper preparation will enable the teacher to make the most effective use of time on the site—and time on field trips is usually limited—as well as to devise ways of keeping up interest. This, I think, must be said: most sites for historical fieldwork, whether they are concerned with prehistoric man, Roman Britain, or industrial archaeology, are intrinsically baffling—one needs to know what to look for. A preliminary survey of the site will indicate how much can be gleaned from a visit for the purposes of the work in hand, and prevent the trip tailing off into irrelevant inquiries and false trails.

Young children, and even older ones, enjoy turning the field trip into a 'treasure hunt' or observation game. I don't personally like the custom of equipping children before any kind of class journey with duplicated lists of questions to be answered—partly because this turns the outing into an exercise, and partly because it imposes too much teacher-control. But certainly note books and pencils can be taken, and the children can be warned to keep their eyes open for interesting observations which they should write down. Rather more direction can be given to this by telling them that they should look particularly for specific items—perhaps dates or initials over the doorways of cottages, perhaps inscriptions on milestones, perhaps firemarks, and so on. Some of the *I-Spy* books published by the Dickens Press suggest the sort of thing they can watch for.

Some care should be taken not to encourage the children merely to collect useless facts for their own sake. There may be an absolute gem of a firemark *en route,* but unless this comes within the context of the project on hand at the moment it is best to ignore it. According to this context, here is a list of some of the questions for which a group might reasonably be prepared before they set out on a field trip:

> There are some old cottages in Mill Lane called Balaclava Cottages. When were they built? If the date wasn't carved over the doors, how would their name give you a clue?
> What were the initials of the builder of Balaclava Cottages?
> Where can you find an Edward VII postbox?
> What was Thompson's the grocer's before it became a grocer's shop?
> When was the Baptist Church built?
> Who paid for the horse-trough to be put in the market-place?
> Where can you see the old spelling of the name of our town?

Once children have grasped what a field trip is all about, this kind of exercise can be dispensed with; even at the beginning, it should be kept as informal as possible. With older children, preparing the class for a journey becomes altogether easier, since they will know the form better.

Early field trips should be confined to the simple objective of getting the children used to seeking information from the things around them. Later, objectives can become more specific, and how this works out in practice can perhaps best be illustrated by accounts of two trips of differing ambitions and complexity.

It has been said that, during the Second World War, there was an airfield every nine miles in Norfolk. One class became interested in this aspect of recent local history, and a project was planned which would culminate in a visit, on an open day, to one of the airfields still operating. Most fields, however, have long since been returned to agricultural use, and in many cases the signs of wartime occupation have been completely obliterated. Using an old set of Ordnance Survey maps (not too old, however, because airfields tended not to be marked until editions published after the war was over), the sites of abandoned fields were found and marked, and it was discovered that the claim of one airfield for every nine miles was not very far out.

The class teacher had found (as a matter of fact, through getting lost on a family outing) that one field quite close to the school was still reasonably well-preserved, though now in use for farming. The perimeter-track, many of the outbuildings, and even the control-tower were still there. Investigation revealed that the buildings left standing were quite safe. The farmer using the site agreed to a class visit provided this took place after the corn had been cut, and before he re-ploughed.

This left ample time for preparation at school. The site was found on maps, and a 2½-inch Ordnance Survey map was obtained on which the airfield, though not marked, was drawn in by the children. A weekend visit to the local pub enabled the teacher to discover that it had been a fighter base, and that a squadron of Hurricanes had been based there, followed later in the war by Meteors. Pictures of these were obtained, and one boy in the class turned up with a balsa wood model of a Hurricane which had been made by his father. By the time the corn was cut on the deserted airfield, the class was well-briefed on the period in time into which it was going to take a glimpse.

In fact, the trip relied heavily upon the imagination. The only things to be seen were the control-tower, with its empty windows staring over a field of burnt cornstalks, the perimeter-track, with its hardstandings now half-hidden by undergrowth, a few Nissen huts, and the base of what had been the station's flagpole. Yet such was the careful preparation that had gone into the visit that the class was well able to sense the busyness, twenty-five years before, of this Norfolk field, with fighters bumping down the slope into the wind, more waiting to turn into the take-off path, and the concrete area by the Nissen huts busy with airmen at work.

Later, back at school, there were detailed plans of the airfield to be drawn, a model to be made, stories to be written, and further investigations into aircraft of the 1939–45 war to be carried out. For once, fathers' stories of what they did in the war gained relevance, and a collection of these was put together. From a few acres of military litter, this class had gained an historical experience.

A second project, this time in Dorset, concerned a stretch of disused railway-line. The line, which used to feed the main London to Weymouth line, was once double-track all the way. By the time the school party visited it, one set of rails had been taken up and the other, though still in place, had clearly not been used for years. On the current edition of the local Ordnance Survey map, however, the line was still shown as operational.

The first stage in the teacher's preparation for a field trip was to study the map closely and see at which points along its route the line could be observed. In a distance of three miles or so, there were several. There were four places at which roads crossed the line, either at level-crossings or by bridges; two stretches of line had roads running alongside them for several hundred yards. Altogether, there were five reasonably good survey points, omitting one of the road crossings where it would have been too dangerous to take a class.

The children—in their last junior school year, and with some experience of this kind of work—then each traced a map of the track, using the 2½-inch Ordnance Survey. They marked in the points at which they would be studying the line. Each child was then provided with a primitive clipboard made of a strawboard offcut and a Bulldog clip. With their map tracings clipped to these, and an extra piece of tracing paper over the top for field notes, the class was equipped to set out.

There was plenty to be seen. Beside one of the level-crossings was a signal-box, with its door removed and some evidence of vandalism inside but still containing enough equipment to make a close study worthwhile. The six or so signal-levers still had metal labels fixed to them showing the signals which they controlled; one group sketched in on their tracings the signalling system. The wheel controlling the level-crossing was still there, although broken, but the children could see how a signalman manning it had a clear view both ways both along the line and up and down the road. At various other survey points, lineside notices were to be seen and noted: gradient-posts, *Whistle* signs, *Trespassers will be prosecuted* notices with the *L, &* and *W* of *L & S W R* mysteriously painted out, mileposts—all these were recorded to be discussed in class later, and to form the basis of further work. The gradient-posts, for example, enabled one group to produce a 'profile' of this stretch of line.

The imaginative side of a project like this should not be ignored. It is all very well to study the leftovers of the past, but unless these can be peopled it is rather like studying the skeletons of Nelson, Napoleon *et al* instead of looking at their personalities. This, of course, is where oral history can again be helpful. One might, with luck, find a local resident who worked at the airfield, or on the railway-line as the case may be. In the latter case, some of the wide range of local railway histories might yield stories of the line's construction and operation, perhaps even with illustrations. Local museums and archives could again be checked for relevant material.

Much of the more detailed fieldwork of the industrial archaeologist is out of range of the school party, though there are, of course, exceptions. Many areas of the country have now been covered in detailed studies of their industrial archaeology, and it is worth combing through these to find out what can be done. Often, however, significant industrial buildings are still in use in new roles, and in these cases permission to visit is usually difficult to obtain, while the value of visits may be in question except to experts. One very useful activity, however, preceded as before by map study, is to take a class to a vantage-point from which they can get a bird's-eye view of their district. It is then possible to trace the development of a village or town with comparative ease: in a village, from the cluster of buildings round the church or green to the straggle of ribbon-development bungalows of the 1930s on the outskirts, and perhaps a group of post-war agricultural workers' council houses; in a town, from the terraced rows of nineteenth-century industrial building to the suburbs of pre-war and post-war development. There was a vogue in the middle of the nineteenth century for 'bird's-eye view' engravings of our major cities, and if one of these can be obtained it will be a source of immense interest.[1]

[1] Try the local museum or County Records Office, or, in the case of a railway town, the British Railways Historical Records Office, 66 Porchester Road, London W2. Photostats of such engravings can often be obtained from these sources for a small fee. For a large bird's-eye view of London, the Summer 1970 issue of *Pictorial Education Quarterly*, published by Evans Brothers, is recommended.

The centres of most towns of any size, particularly of those which have declined in importance, often amply repay close study. Today, a town centre is often obscured because new traffic patterns have made it no longer the hub of local life; similarly, market-places have declined as markets were set up on new sites on the edge of towns. In terms of contemporary life, the centre of a town can be almost unnoticed, but its significance in the past can often be rediscovered by fieldwork. A couple of examples will illustrate this. The town of Blandford, in Dorset, has a fine town centre, formerly a market-place, which has been successively by-passed by the developments of the past century or so. First, the railway station was built on the edge of the town, to the north-east, and since the railway's main business was agricultural traffic this moved the town's business emphasis in that direction as well. Later, at the outbreak of the First World War, a large military camp was built on the hills to the north-west, again turning Blandford's attention away from its centre. Finally, with the railway closed and the market abandoned, a one-way traffic system designed to help on its way the coastward-bound summer traffic from the Midlands has turned the centre of the town into a fume-laden conveyor-belt. Nowadays, you have to try to blot out the traffic, and then if you stand back you can see the market square as it must have been at the height of its glory—with the church and a fine Corn Exchange dominating one side, flanked by the substantial commercial premises of the banks, the lawyers' offices, the agricultural merchants' shops, and so on.

It happens that documentation on the recent past of Blandford is plentiful—mainly because the town was virtually destroyed by fire in the eighteenth century—and consequently the market-place makes an ideal subject for a modelling project. Blandford's past as a garrison town suggests themes for imaginative work with which the model can be peopled.

A few miles away, on the Dorset/Hampshire border, is the village of Cranborne. Whereas Blandford is steadily being throttled by road traffic, Cranborne has been put into a decline by twentieth-century (and even earlier) neglect. The railway passed it by, and there is no major road within miles. As a result, the centre of Cranborne, a market square less impressive than Blandford's but easier to see as a market square because less has happened over the years to obscure it, is more or less as it must have been when the village was a thriving market centre 150 years ago. There is a slight threat to preservation of this backwater from a 'garden centre' at the big house on the outskirts of the village, but in general enough can be seen to indicate how closely-knit a community Cranborne was until fairly recently. The Primitive Methodist Chapel has become an art gallery, the police station a private house, and so on, but they can still be recognised.

We have now moved away from pure history, whatever pure history might be, into the realm of settlement studies, and this again illustrates the value of this particular approach to history when it can be absorbed into an integrated curriculum. With older children, at the top of the junior school or in a middle school, the study in detail of the development of a fairly small town (or of its decline, as in the case of Cranborne and many similar market towns in rural areas) is an ideal subject for the integrated approach, either with one teacher or as a team teaching project. The reasons why population centres shift are rarely exclusive to one discipline: geographical history, scientific and technological history, as well as pure history, play a part. Some aspects of these changes are beyond the concept range of junior or middle school children, of course, and will form the basis of later studies at CSE or GCE level; but it is important that the teacher should appreciate them to enable him to discover the form which projects with his own class can take. In any case, many of these changes are capable of interpretation within the terms of junior school history as they have been discussed in this book.

I return to Swindon for an illustration of how a town can develop and how the factors in its development can be put to use in the history studies of a junior school. Before the arrival of the Great Western Railway, Swindon was a small market town on the edge of the Wiltshire/Berkshire downs. (The old market-place in Old Town, with its characteristic range of buildings—Corn Market, square, inn and banks—can still be seen.) It must have been a rural backwater in the real sense; no main roads passed near, and even today if you travel north-east from Old Town you very quickly come to remote downland country, in spite of the fact that the new M4 runs, skilfully concealed, through it.

It is interesting to speculate on what might have happened to Swindon if the Great Western Railway from London to Bristol had taken a more northerly route; probably Swindon would today be like Cranborne, a victim of increasing centralisation of population and trade. As it happened, however, the line of the GWR was planned a mile or so to the north of Swindon Old Town, though this in itself was not enough to change the town's destiny.

In the early days of railways, staging-posts were needed at fairly frequent intervals in order to re-coal and water the locomotives and to allow 'comfort' and refreshment stops for the passengers. Swindon is very roughly half-way between Paddington and Bristol, but in fact Steventon (which in fact was at one early stage used for the purpose) or Didcot or Challow could have served equally well. The probably apocryphal story of the choice of Swindon is that the creators of the GWR, Daniel Gooch and Isambard Kingdom Brunel, were surveying the route to find a site for the railway's main stopping-place, and also for its engine factory and repair yard, and eventually, unable to decide which of a number of available sites was most suitable, threw a stone. Where it landed was to be the engineering headquarters and focal point of the new line. The stone fell at Swindon.

It is far more likely, of course, that the landowners at Swindon were more amenable and less demanding than those elsewhere. But certainly the choice of Swindon was pretty arbitrary; all the raw materials for the engine and carriage works had to be brought from the Midlands or South Wales, together with much of the skilled labour. It is a tribute to the determination of Victorian industry, however, in spite of the importation of skills from elsewhere, that the GWR was able to base a highly successful and productive establishment in such alien human as well as geographical surroundings. (This is, incidentally, a reflection of that particular Victorian skill for creating viable labour forces from unpromising material. The new employment opportunities in Victorian times provided by the railways, by the Post Office, by police forces and so on were taken up by unskilled and largely uneducated people who were given vocational education through their work and *esprit de corps* largely by such devices as uniforms and the introduction of recognisable scales of pay and avenues of promotion. Unimaginable as this may seem today, the new Victorian institutions were progressive and benevolent employers, and there is particular evidence of this in respect of the GWR in the numerous 'loyal addresses' presented by its employees to its senior officials and directors on a number of occasions. Some of these are exhibited in the Swindon Railway Museum.)

So the railway came to Swindon, and the railway created a new town which for many years appeared on maps as New Swindon. Beside the railway works, the GWR built a model estate for its workers which still stands: neat cottages for family men, a lodging-house for bachelors and temporary workers (subsequently a Methodist Church and now the Railway Museum), a church (St Mark's), a Mechanics' Institute, and so on. For a century, until the early 1960s when, with the disappearance of steam, the railway works began to be run down, nearly every man in Swindon who was not involved in service industries worked 'inside' —in the long sheds where locomotives were made, where skills and pride in them were almost legendary.

It was the impending Second World War that brought changes to Swindon. In the 1930s, the Vickers Supermarine Company established a factory and airfield at South Marston, just outside the town, where a large part of Britain's fighter force was made. Industrialists of the 1930s, it will be noted, were canny enough to choose an area where technological tradition and metal-working skills were already strong. Following the establishment of the aircraft works, supporting industries —notably electronics—moved in, and these gradually began to take over from the now traditional work 'inside'. By the time the aircraft industry began to pull out—round about the mid-1950s—local electronic skills were able to stand on their own feet, and meanwhile the designation of Swindon as a London overspill area had resulted in the inflow of new trades and new, mainly light, industries. Typical Swindon industries today are electronics sub-contracting, warehousing for such national firms as W. H. Smith, the manufacture of domestic articles, and so on. The railway works is virtually dead, and the airfield at South Marston shows a shadow of its former activity.

Such is the history of industry in Swindon. What can be gained from it for use in environmental history projects?

Almost every Swindon family can claim members with a direct relationship with one or other of the town's different phases of development. Grandparents will remember the days when almost everyone who worked worked 'inside', and there will be stories to tell of the heavy industry which now seems quite out of place in this Wiltshire countryside. Surnames will often be indicative here; an influx of Welsh names is prominent, dating from the early days of Swindon as a railway centre. Other families will have moved into the area in the pre-war years, from aircraft industry centres like Weybridge and Southampton. Others again will have come after the war, to help set up the new Swindon of light industry. An occasional family will still be able to trace itself back to Faringdon or Shrivenham or one of the other villages close by, having moved into Swindon for the better wages paid in the railway works when agriculture was declining but local industry was thirsty for manpower. All this can come to light in a 'family tree' type of project as outlined in Chapter 2.

In terms of fieldwork, there is still plenty to be seen. On the western edge of the town, the long profile of the railway works is still there, stretching out towards Wootton Bassett with an attendant string of now largely deserted sidings. Although the railway itself is, of course, not to be explored, much of its significance in the life of Swindon can be recaptured in the Railway Museum in the centre of the town. The airfield at South Marston is still accessible. Some stretches—now dry, but still discernible—of the Kennet and Avon canal, remnants of an earlier and rather abortive chapter in Swindon's communications history, can still be explored. And from Liddington Hill, to the south-east, the whole town can be overlooked, and the different phases of its development traced.

I have written at such length about Swindon in order to illustrate how, even in a town with little 'history' in terms of monumental brasses or medieval churches or ancient monuments (though in fact there are plenty of the latter within easy reach on the downs outside the town), there is plenty of scope for historical exploration. The surprising thing is that when I was teaching there, some fifteen years ago, no one thought of putting the town's recent history to use in the classroom. Things are, I don't doubt, different now, but in those days history continued firmly to be a matter of Magna Carta and Alfred and Stonehenge and so on. Yet on our doorstep (and, had we but known it, dying before our eyes) was a heritage of industrial skill and a community way of life which we could have studied then 'for real' and which can now only be re-created through such artificial, museum-centred devices as industrial archaeological societies. Yet all that was needed, at that time, was to take children out to look at their environment.

Such vague generalisations are all very well, of course, but something more specific is needed before a teacher dare venture forth with a class. To conclude this chapter on fieldwork, then, let me summarise some of the points I have made earlier in the chapter.

In fieldwork with juniors, objectives should be limited and precise. The teacher should not be tempted to overload the aims of a trip out simply because the arrangements may have been complicated; far better to return with a small accomplishment than with a haze of undigested observation. Preparation, in the light of the objectives, should be thorough and careful. While many teachers will not want to specify *to the children* the object of the work, they should be aware of this themselves, and their preparation should be always in the light of the object. Similarly, follow-up work, whether this takes the form of creative writing, drama, model-making, painting, or whatever, should be directed. Unless the teacher keeps control of what the children are doing, environmental history can all too easily break up into a kind of general, woolly survey of 'the olden days'. Finally, every opportunity should be taken to cross-reference new discoveries and new topics with what has gone before, whether in earlier local history projects or in general history studies. Throughout the study of Swindon, for example, the teacher should expect to have to refer back to the development of railways in general.

Chapter 5

History from traditional culture

There are not so many first-hand sources of history that we can afford to ignore any that do exist. This chapter is concerned with the use which can be made in school of the remnants (in some cases, living remnants) of traditional and folk culture. Most of history must of necessity be studied from printed sources, and sources which offer experience in other dimensions are doubly to be welcomed. What we have left of traditional culture can bring to vibrant life such topics as the effect of the Enclosure Acts upon rural life, the industrialisation of the former cottage skills of spinning and weaving, the influence of increasing urbanisation, and so on.

I have found, though, that in introducing the idea of using traditional sources to teachers who know little about them it is necessary to begin with an apologia. It is not easy for anyone brought up, as most of us were, to sing devitalised, dehumanised schoolroom versions of folksongs, and to hear drawing-room versions sung by Grand Hotel baritones, to approach the use of folksong as a respectable historical source without some diffidence, and the same kind of diffidence must restrain the enthusiasm of those to whom folksong has in recent years become associated with such pop music figures as Joan Baez, Bob Dylan and Simon and Garfunkel.

As will be seen, however, I shall not be dealing in this chapter with the hackneyed songs of the *Early One Morning* variety, nor with so-called 'contemporary' folksongs. Nor, indeed, will I be dealing with folksong alone. The repertory of traditional culture includes, as well as song, the whole range of artistic activity from dance through drama to ritual of an almost religious sort. We are wrong to hinder children's access to these things, if only because, to quote just two examples, the Padstow May Day ceremony and the ballad of *The Babes in the Wood* are two of the oldest cultural manifestations we have.

In many respects, education has served traditional culture pretty badly. I have referred in an earlier chapter to the fake May Day ceremonies still indulged in by many schools in the belief that they are keeping traditional culture going; the widespread adoption of traditional crafts as school exercises (often using, in these days, *plastic* straw!) is another example; but the most grisly testimony to the misuse of folk tradition for educational purposes—and one that still corrupts us today—is provided by the record of what happened to folksong when it was taken up at the turn of the century by the then Board of Education.

The establishment of a national education system had created a need for a considerable repertoire of songs for use in schools which would be within the compass both of the children and of teachers who had received no formal musical training and whose musical ability was often limited to picking out simple unison hymn melodies on the piano. The work of folksong collectors like Cecil Sharp, Sabine Baring-Gould, Frank Kidson and others filled this vacuum admirably; here was a store of songs, many of which had simple, repetitive melody lines, which had been created for unaccompanied singing, and which were readily available. No wonder that in its 1905 edition of the *Handbook of Suggestions for the Consideration of Teachers* the Board was enthusiastic in its recommendation of folksong for schools, though it had not yet quite sorted out the difference between songs from the oral tradition and composed nationalistic pieces like *Rule Britannia.*

'National or folk songs,' said the *Handbook,* 'are the expression in the idiom of the people of their joys and sorrows, their unaffected patriotism, their zest for sport and the simple pleasures of a country life. Such music is the early and spontaneous uprising of artistic power in a nation, and the ground on which all national music is built up; folksongs are the true classics of a people, and their survival, so often by tradition alone, proves that their appeal is direct and lasting.'

There followed some advice on the selection of folksongs for use in schools. Care must be taken, said the *Handbook,* in making a choice, because some songs were unsuitable 'either in words or in compass'. Generally, the message of the Board of Education was that the music was more important than the words—advice which, indeed, reflected the view of the pioneer collector Cecil Sharp and most of his colleagues.

The result was that the vast mass of song rediscovered by Sharp and his fellow researchers was fed, without much respect for its quality, as raw material into the educational machine. Music was rearranged and refashioned to suit the limited accommodation of school pianos and teachers' musical ability. Words were shamelessly edited so as to turn many sensitive and beautiful songs into rhyming gibberish of the 'fal-de-lal-the-day' type. Many songs whose sentiments did not entirely fit in with the Board of Education's image of 'the simple pleasures of a country life' were suppressed altogether and disappeared from view for two generations or more. The legacy of tidied-up tunes and prettied-up words bequeathed by this process, which has persisted until our own day, is as unrepresentative as could be of the power and strength and durability of traditional song. It has been responsible for the haze of Strawberry Fairism through which too many adults today, as a result of the false images fed to them at school, view the history of the countryside. In fact, country life at about the time when Sharp was collecting and the Board of Education issuing its hopeful words about 'simple pleasures', was at a lower ebb, in terms of subsistence as well as pleasure, than it had been for a century and possibly longer. The more active members of the rural population had fled to the towns in retreat from the great agricultural depression of the last decades of the nineteenth century, leaving rural life to the elderly and infirm to guard their roofs against corrosion and their hearts against collapse for want of hope.

Fortunately, the folklore movement as a whole has recovered from this unpromising start. The tendency among recent collectors has been to by-pass their predecessors and go back to original sources. As a result, we are as well equipped today as we shall ever be to pass on to children something of the flavour of traditional entertainments and pastimes: seasonal rituals, folk drama and dancing as well as folksong itself.

In fact, junior school children are very close to the oral tradition, because they are the inheritors of the last repository of a living oral tradition in Britain. This is the play-rhyme in its various forms: the rhymes to be heard in any playground in season as an accompaniment to those incredibly complicated skipping and ball-bouncing routines so beloved by junior school girls, the ritual chants used to choose someone to be 'it', and the street songs which are themselves a fusion of folk-song, yesterday's pops, and hymn-tunes. What makes these children's songs interesting is that they continue today, absorbing current social trends and discarding these successively in favour of new ones, without the help of collectors or revivalists, the last surviving models of the process by which all traditional culture has been communicated down the centuries.

Thus the traditional songs and chants of the playground have celebrated in turn most of the popular heroes and villains of the day—Baden-Powell, Crippen, Kitchener, Hitler and Mussolini, Gary Cooper, Diana Dors and the Beatles, to name but a varied few. Bringing them inside from the playground forms the basis of an attractive junior school project for a number of reasons: it demonstrates what adults know but children find hard to accept—that today is, as we live it, already passing into history; it provides a useful link between generations which can serve to soften up parents and grandparents for the more demanding contributions which may be asked for later on; it makes children aware of the natural time-scale afforded by the generations; and the interest aroused overflows easily into other subject areas. Perhaps most valuable of all, it shows that the study of a subject in some depth need not be a dull academic, book-ridden exercise.

Children's games, songs, rituals and *lingua franca* have been closely observed and recorded in a series of books by Peter and Iona Opie, and these are valuable for reference; but the most useful reference for a project of this sort is the repertoire of the children themselves.[1] Once the children discover that they are the sole possessors of something interesting and apparently valuable to an adult, they will rack their brains and their parents' and grandparents' memories for remnants of half-forgotten routines to contribute.

In my experience, the resources of one's own class can provide a fair stock of material to start off with. In the course of three days, I once collected from a class of ten-year-olds in a suburban Kent school no less than twenty-three routines of various kinds still in current use among that particular group of children. They varied from mere fragments like:

> Two little sausages frying in a pan,
> One went pop and the other went bang.

to enormously long quasi-dramatic rituals which were, in fact, tests of skipping ability analogous of the folksongs of the *Twelve Days of Christmas* and *Green Grow the Rushes* type which were sung as feats of memory.

The facility with which children learn such complicated routines is staggering to the teacher who is used, in these days, to making such minimal demands on their memory. Among my sample of twenty-three rhymes, for example, was the following intricate ritual (a standard work of the playground, as I found out later) which achieved something of the status of folk drama. It was performed by a group of six or so girls, a fresh member of the group stepping into the turning rope at the beginning of each new verse.

> Queenie, Queenie Caroline
> Dipped her hair in the turpentine.
> The turpentine began to shine,
> Queenie, Queenie Caroline.

> (Susan Warner[2]) sat on the shore,
> She had children, three or four,
> The eldest one is twenty-four
> And she's getting married to the boy next door.
> How many children will they have?
> One, two, three, four, five, six, seven, eight, nine, etc. . . . .

[1] The Opies' works in this field are listed in the Source list.
[2] The name of a member of the group is fitted in here.

What will they live on?
Salt, mustard, vinegar, pepper, etc. . . .

What will they live in?
House, flat, pigsty, lavatory, etc. . . .

. . . and so on. By this time, the floodgates were opened. Children who had moved from other districts were reporting local variants which they had learned at their previous schools, and the first offerings from home were coming in. We soon had the beginnings of an anthology in sound of the children's songs of twenty, forty, sixty years ago, to which we were able to add later from printed and recorded sources.

There were also interesting sidelines to be explored as time and inclination might permit. Who *was* Queenie Caroline? Who was Lord Kitchener, who turned up in a rhyme contributed on a crumpled, closely-written piece of paper sent in by a grandma? Another notable feature of the children's researches was the number of children's variants of one-time popular songs, including one which began *Oh, Them Golden Kippers* of which, unfortunately, only the one line had survived.

The rewriting of popular songs is a continuing children's (and, of course, adult) custom. Many people who were, like me, just starting school before the last war will remember the playground version of the popular song of the time *Under the Spreading Chestnut Tree* :

> Underneath the spreading chestnut tree,
> Mr Chamberlain said to me:
> 'If you want to get your gas-mask free,
> Join the blinkin' ARP.'[3]

A journalist visiting Ontario in the summer of 1971 reported hearing a group of eight-year-old girls singing a bloodthirsty, long hot summer version of the Kentucky mountain song *On Top of Old Smoky* which began:

> On top of Old Smoky, all covered with mud,
> I spied my poor teacher, all covered with blood.
> A knife in her stomach, an axe on her head,
> I formed the impression my teacher was dead . . .[4]

A related field which is worth exploring, particularly if parents can be involved, is that of street games of the hopscotch and tipcat variety, which, if the people who regularly write to *The Times* about them are to be believed, are fast disappearing. It is probably true that reach-me-down versions of adult games have superseded many of the traditional street games, but hopscotch is still familiar enough, to judge by the

[3] As Norman Longmate points out in his social history of the Second World War, *How We Lived Then* (Hutchinson, 1971), this rhyme was inaccurate as well as unpatriotic; everyone, in the ARP or not, got a free gas-mask.
[4] *The Times Educational Supplement,* 9 July 1971.

number of chalked grids one still sees on pavements, and I suspect that many games have proved more resistant than we tend to think. Chapbooks of the eighteenth century often contain accounts of these games, and it is interesting to try them out with a group of children to see if they still have any appeal today. Nor are ritual party games like *Ring-a-ring-o'-roses* to be despised; to tell children of the origins of this rhyme at the time of the Great Plague is an unfailing way of capturing their interest.

Any or all of these topics provide an introduction to the use of folksong itself as a history source. Here, thanks to the wave of enthusiasm among modern collectors, there is an almost endless archive to be explored, readily available in print or on records.

The roots of folksong are diverse. Much—including the songs of the great pastoral tradition of which *Early One Morning* and *Richard of Taunton Dene* are the schoolroom survivals—is the iceberg-tip of a strain of balladry reaching back into the Middle Ages and perhaps beyond. Into this category fall a great number of almost classical songs which turn up in an infinite number of variants not only throughout the British Isles but also in the mountain states of western North America, in Newfoundland and Nova Scotia, in Australia and South Africa. Added to these are a number of traditional songs which achieved printed form during the late eighteenth and early nineteenth centuries, in the heyday of the broadsides or ballad-sheets sold in the streets and at markets and fairs. The broadside-printers—and every town of any size had its local printer who produced ballad-sheets as a bread-and-butter activity to fill in time between commissioned work—extended the traditional material by using local or national events as the subject of further songs. (Some, indeed, are said to have been subsidised by Government funds to enable them to produce stirring jingoistic broadsides aimed at stimulating recruitment to the forces.) By the end of the eighteenth century, the broadside occupied a position in national culture roughly equivalent to today's popular press, and some ballads (notably one commemorating the murder of Maria Marten in the Red Barn) achieved quite astonishing circulations of several millions. As in today's papers, crime, personalities, rather false patriotism and sex were the main standbys of the broadside.

A third element was added to the folksong mixture with the development of the music-hall during the nineteenth century. Some broadside material found its way into the halls to begin a new life there, and in the early days there was some traffic the other way. The repertoire of the country singers whose songs were collected in the early years of the present century included items drawn from all three lines of descent.

In using this material in the classroom, it's important, I think, to be honest; folksong is no longer the popular song of yesterday. There are isolated pockets in Britain where traditional songs are still sung instinctively, without influence from revival, but these are few. Even when

Sharp and his colleagues were collecting, seventy years ago, their sources were usually the oldest inhabitants; so it is generally true to say that traditional songs have not been sung habitually for something like 120 years. Even so, there is an important exception to this in the industrial song to which reference will be made later, while it is always worth following up traditional songs which are known to have been collected locally. Collections of folksongs normally contain a note of the name of the original singer and the place where the song was collected, and in some areas descendants of the original singers can still be traced. John R. Baldwin, revisiting between 1966 and 1969 the haunts of the Wiltshire collector Alfred Williams, found a number of family links with the singers who had sung to Williams fifty or more years before. If it is possible for a collector from outside to find these links, how much more easy it must be for local people and, in particular, for local schools.[5]

When we come to examine the half-world between folk and popular song—a type which Sharp derided as 'vulgar street music'—local tradition becomes more marked and historical value more evident. One of the characteristics of recent folksong collecting has been the rediscovery of local songs, often with an industrial significance. Some areas—including London, Liverpool, the Northumberland and Durham coalfields, and the cotton-spinning towns of Lancashire—have been particularly well explored, revealing many songs apparently exclusive to their particular areas as well as local variants of nationally-known songs.

The material collected in the coalfields of the north-east gives an idea of the value of regional song in history studies. In fact, Tyneside and its hinterland seems always to have been strong in regional song; it is from this area that such well-known pieces as *The Keel Row, The Sandgate Girl's Lament, Will Ye Buy My Fresh Fish?*, and *Blow the Wind Southerly* come. These, however, are of earlier origin; the songs of the coalfields seem to have developed as a result of the coming together of a number of different influences: the importation of Irish labour, which brought a new repertoire of tunes; the development of working-men's clubs from about 1850 onwards which stimulated singing as a pastime; and the increasing spread of trade unionism, which gave the miners something to sing about. The twin themes of most coalfield songs are disaster and the class struggle.

Before the days of compulsory workers' insurance and the payment of death or disablement benefits by the state, the death or injury of a breadwinner meant not only personal tragedy for his family but also, often, financial ruin, homelessness and near-starvation. The only money available, unless his employers were in particularly generous mood or decided to pay up to quieten gossip about their own culpability, for the family of a man killed or seriously injured at work was that collected by a whip-round among his workmates—a custom which developed, as

[5] See the *Folk Music Journal*, Volume 1 No 5, 1969. (English Folk Dance and Song Society.)

the working-men's clubs were introduced, into the idea of a 'benefit night'. It was against this background that there came into being a number of songs composed following mine accidents, which were, to judge from the records, horrifyingly common in the late nineteenth century.

The north-east had a particularly prolific composer in Thomas Armstrong, whose songs—set to traditional tunes—included not only disaster ballads but also humorous pieces attacking the popular targets of his audiences (mine overseers, racketeering shopkeepers and beer-watering publicans, and the School Board Man or attendance officer). In February 1872 seventy-two miners died in a gas explosion at Trimdon Grange Colliery in County Durham. Within a day or two, Armstrong had composed a benefit song for their families, and was singing it in the local clubs. The second of his five simply and directly worded verses went:

> Men and boys left home that morning
> For to earn their daily bread;
> Little thought before the evening
> They'd be numbered with the dead.
> Let us think of Mrs Burnett—
> Once had sons and now has none—
> With the Trimdon Grange explosion
> Joseph, George and James are gone.

Although the Trimdon Grange Colliery closed in 1968, the explosion is still remembered in the village; the song, available on a number of records, brings the event out of the local history books into life.

The development of trade unionism in the coalfield, too, left a legacy of songs, some shot through with bitterness against the mine-owners and others reserving the miner's greatest contempt for non-union labour. The employers' response to the formation of a union branch was often to import blackleg labour from outside, and it was this that inspired the song—also from the Durham coalfield—of *The Blackleg Miner*. The threats to the blacklegs were explicit:

> And don't go near the Seghill mine.
> Across the way they stretch a line
> To catch the throat and break the spine
> Of the dirty blackleg miner.[6]

The combination of folksong evidence with that from other sources can often prove effective. It is inevitable, of course, that the selection of material has to remain with the teacher, and this makes it all the more important that sources should be chosen carefully. Some years ago,

[6] For a full account of industrial folksong, with particular reference to the north-east coalfield disaster songs and Thomas Armstrong, see *Folk-song in England* by A. L. Lloyd (Lawrence and Wishart, 1967).

running a project on the Victorian age with a group of ten and eleven-year-olds, I found it difficult to persuade them that, a century before, they would probably have been at work. Their only background reading had suggested to them that normal life for children of their age in Victorian England was not too different—apart from styles of dress and modes of transport—from their own. I played the class a record of a song from Teesdale which I thought would be testimony enough. It was *Fourpence a Day*, which begins:

> The ores are waiting in the tubs, and snow's upon the fell.
> Canny folks are sleeping yet, but lead is right to sell.
> Come, ye little washer lads, come, let's away:
> We're bound down to slavery for fourpence a day.

The children weren't too sure about this; with more critical ability than I'd credited them with, they suspected the song as propagandist. Or, to use their words, 'That's just a song, isn't it?' Fortunately, I had other sources up my sleeve, and what finally convinced them on my point was, oddly enough, a passage from the autobiography of the early Labour leader Tom Mann, which goes to show that teaching sources are to be found in the most unlikely places. While the words of the folksong had not rung true, Tom Mann's did:

> 'I started work down the mine in the air courses. A number of men and boys were always at this work: the duties were to make and keep in order small roads or "courses" to convey the air to take respective workings in the mines. These air courses were only three feet high and wide, and my work was to take away the "mullock", coal or dirt that the man would require taken from him as he worked away at "heading" a new road, or repairing an existing one.
>
> 'For this removal there were boxes known down the mine as "dans", about two feet six inches long and eighteen inches wide and of a similar depth, with an iron ring strongly fixed at each end. I had to draw the box along, not on rails; it was built sledge-like, and each boy had a belt and chain . . . Donkey work it certainly was. The boys were stripped to the waist, and as there were only candles enough for one each, and these could not be carried, but had to be fixed at each end of the stages, the boy had to crawl on hands and toes dragging his load along in worse than Egyptian darkness. Many a time did I actually lie down groaning as a consequence of the heavy strain on the loins, especially when the road was wet and "clayey" causing much resistance to the load being dragged.'[7]

---

[7] *Tom Mann's Memoirs*, Labour Publishing Company, 1923; reprinted by MacGibbon and Kee, 1967.

Tom Mann was ten years old at the time; the year was 1866.

The moral to be drawn from this story of the children's suspicion of the folksong and need for confirmation from more documentary evidence is, I think, that song is better used as background than as an introduction to a topic. It takes a degree of sophistication to appreciate that the words of a song can convey a bitter or horrific message rather than a pleasant one, and children have not had the experience that adults have had in the use of juxtaposed images in film and on television.

It would be pleasant, but it is unfortunately not practicable within the scope of this book, to give an annotated list of traditional material and its place in the history syllabus, topic by topic or area by area. It can be said, though, that some topics and some areas are very densely covered, and here traditional sources can be very valuable indeed. Fishing on the east coast, seafaring generally, agriculture, hunting and other country pursuits including cock-fighting, prize-fighting, press gangs and recruitment for the army and such national triumphs and disasters as the Battle of Abraham Heights, Waterloo, the Great Fire of London and the sinking of the Titanic are all well-represented in folksong; geographically, most of the rural south of England, the north-east coast of Scotland, Yorkshire and the south-west, in addition to the areas mentioned earlier, figure prominently in standard folksong collections, a number of which are listed at the end of this book. Other sources of help for the teacher include the secretaries of local folksong clubs and branches of the English Folk Dance and Song Society.

There is an example of how traditional singing can prove a valuable link with an area's past in the story of Bob and Ron Copper, two Sussex cousins with a long tradition of family singing behind them. It is a moving story, and a tragic one. The Coppers farmed the land round Rottingdean, near Brighton, for generations, and in fact the family was the source of a large collection of songs made early in this century by Lucy Broadwood. Events between the wars, however, drove the Coppers on hard times. There was an agricultural depression, accompanied at the same time by a thirst for building land. The land the Coppers had farmed was sold for housing. Bob Copper has written:

'My father Jim and his brother John had both started their working lives, as had their father before them, as shepherd boys at the age of eleven years, on these windswept hills overlooking the English Channel. When in later years they saw the grass growing rank from neglect, and, far worse, watched the ever-encroaching tide of new houses and bungalows creeping further and further back into the downland, you can imagine how they felt. I remember one evening as Dad and I stood at the back of the village looking down the valley, which seemed to be breaking out in a sporadic rash of red-brick bungalows, he turned to me and said, "I don't know what your old grand-daddy would say, boy, if he could see this lot.

Houses, 'ouses, 'ouses; y'know that makes me prostrate with dismal." '8

From that point on, the Copper family's songs became their only link with their past, and the Copper family still clings to its legacy of songs, a number of which have been recorded. If I were teaching in Rottingdean, or indeed anywhere along the stretch of coastal downland between Brighton and Eastbourne which used to be the Southdown sheep country and which has suffered so grievously from bungaloid development, I should want to make sure that the children both heard and learned to sing the songs produced when the land they live on was a better place.

I mention singing particularly, because folksong is one historical source that you can actually enjoy in a positive way. 'Voice and ear,' wrote Robert Frost, 'are left at a loss what to do with the ballad until supplied with the tune it was written to go with.' He might have added that folksong never really comes home until one sings it oneself. Most folksong is eminently singable—and I do not, of course, mean from careful arrangements practised and polished in music lessons. Children will readily learn them from records with no help in the way of formal teaching. They should be fairly familiar with songs before they do any work on them, and one way of achieving this is to play records as background music, for incidental listening in periods when quiet is not needed, and perhaps at the beginning or end of assembly. The pop music world has demonstrated how enjoyment of simple music and a thirst for more can be created by constant repetition, and teachers need not be afraid that they are debasing traditional material by fostering it in this way; after all, folksong owes its survival to the oral transmission of oft-repeated songs.

There must, however, be a word of warning for teachers intending to use folksong records in the classroom. Record manufacturers do not produce these discs specifically for schools, and since the current trend —quite rightly—is to avoid the Bowdlerisation of texts which damaged so many early collections, there are few albums which do not contain at least one item which teachers may find unsuitable for school use. I personally wish that teachers could be more liberal about the material they present to children, but at the same time there is no denying that however liberally-minded teachers might themselves be they have to take account of the real or supposed vulnerabilities of head teachers, local education authorities and parents. The best advice one can give is that, before a teacher uses any folksong material in class, he should listen to it carefully with the critical ear likely to be applied by any of the potential censors. It is also as well to remember that words which sound innocuous in one's own home may sound very different in front of a

8 Sleeve note to record LP 1002, *Bob and Ron Copper,* English Folk Dance and Song Society, 1963.

class. As David Holbrook has written, of a particular record, 'teachers should be warned that some of the love-songs are outspoken, with Johnnies getting into bed with their pit-boots on, and if they let these go they must be strong enough to take the reaction'.

Closely linked with folksong are the few remnants of folk drama which have survived, usually as a result of dedicated preservation. Some of these are in the form of folksong fragments, like the *Cheshire Souling Song,* the *Pace-Egging Song,* smatterings of wassail songs and a number of 'calling-on' songs associated with rapper dancing, particularly in the north of England. The best-known material of this sort is the Padstow May Day ritual, and a number of other west country towns, including Helston and Minehead, still have revived ceremonies of this type. The archetypal folk-play is, of course, *St George and the Dragon,* which still survives in a variety of forms and is performed here and there by mummers, notably at Christmas-time (at Bampton-in-the-Bush, Oxford-shire, and Northleach, Gloucestershire) but also in one or two places at Easter, Whitsun or All Souls' Tide. Again, local members of the English Folk Dance and Song Society are probably the best source of information and help.

The basic script of *St George and the Dragon,* which is fairly freely available,[9] can be used for school drama either as it stands or with additional material. As with many folksongs, the play was often adapted to bring in local allusions and well-known local figures, and the form of the script is so loose that this is easily done. While giving children a basic formula to work on, *St George and the Dragon* enables them also to add something of their own.

Although many traditional customs have been revived in recent years, far more have disappeared, and it would be an excellent achievement if a school were able to bring about the rediscovery of local customs. This seems to have happened, almost spontaneously, at the Sussex down-land village of Alciston, where children and young people gather at noon on Good Friday for skipping in the yard of the Rose Inn, using a long rope provided by the landlord. The participants walk to Alciston across the hills from Newhaven and Seaford, following a custom which until a few years ago was kept up only by a handful of ageing eccentrics. It has been suggested that the Good Friday skip is a survival of the primitive belief in tramping the ground to make the crops grow, but I suspect that the Alciston ceremony is of much more recent origin. How-ever, it is certainly a flourishing ritual today, and very impressive it is to stand in Alciston village early on a Good Friday morning and see the long lines of walkers straggling down the downland paths.

Books of antiquarian jottings, though usually dull reading, can be the source of useful information about local customs. One ceremony rescued from the obscurity of such a volume (in fact, a collection of traditional material by the Lancashire historian Harland) is the strange ritual of

[9] See source list.

Droylsden Wakes, in which a man and a woman, sitting on a cart, 'were engaged with spinning-wheels, spinning flax in the olden style, and conducting a rustic dialogue in limping verse, after which they collected contributions from spectators'. This is clearly an urban version of souling or mumming, carried to Droylsden at the Industrial Revolution and adapted to the 'wakes' holiday pattern. To take another example, it is clear from a book on Dorset customs[10] that Shrove Tuesday was formerly an occasion in Dorset (and Wiltshire) for a similar singing-and-collecting activity. There are reports from several parts of the county of parties of small boys going round the houses to beg bread and cheese or pieces of pancake. A number of variants are given to the verse sung on these visits, a typical one being:

> I be come a-shriving
> For a little pancake
> A bit o' bread o' your baking
> Or a little truckle cheese of your own making.
> If you give me a little, I'll ask no more.
> If you don't give me nothing, I'll rattle your door.

Fists, saucepans or lumps of wood would then be hammered on the door of the unfortunate host. Customs of this sort are certainly worth investigating—though perhaps in this case actual revival, unless some modification were introduced, might not make for local popularity.

It is very easy—and this applies particularly to traditional custom-hunting but also to the use of all traditional material—to become absorbed in the pursuit of the picturesque, and thus to make the same mistake as the Board of Education in 1905 with its emphasis on 'the simple pleasures of a country life'. One must be careful to offset the evidence of the seasonal humanitarianism of gentry and farmers at Christmas-time and after harvest with the equally common evidence of their insensitivity, if not cruelty, at other times. Antiquarian interests, usually centred on the rectory or the Big House, were unlikely to reflect a true picture of country life, and for the darker side one has to go to sources like the Hammonds, to Cobbett, and to the records of, for example, health authorities. Country writers in general tend to emphasise the 'rural bliss' aspect of country life; one notable exception was Ralph Wightman, whose books—in particular his guide-book to Dorset[11]—should be read for a more balanced view. Equally, of course, it would be wrong to depend for sources of information about urban life entirely on such writers as Dickens, Mayhew and Ruskin. For some reason probably buried deep in the British psychology (and still evident) there has been a tendency to romanticise the countryside and denigrate city life, ignoring both the less romantic aspects of the former and the brighter side of the latter.

[10] *Dorsetshire Folklore*, by J. S. Udal, London 1922; reprinted 1970 by Toucan Press, Guernsey.
[11] *Portrait of Dorset*, by Ralph Wightman. (Robert Hale, 1953.)

Chapter 6

Postscript

In the end, the basic challenge to the teacher of history—certainly at the junior or middle school level, and ideally at any level short of higher academic study—is the problem of making contacts between pupils and past: of giving children something of the feeling of what it was like to be living in 1945 or 1918 or 1815 or whenever. Only if this feeling can be put across can the children go on to understand the behaviour and attitudes of the past, and only if this understanding is achieved can history ever become more than a sterile study.

It has been my argument throughout this book that we have a better chance of making contact with the children's immediately preceding generations than with the Britons of the Roman occupation or those of the Beaker Age. But precisely because it is easier—precisely because the points of contact are more easily recognised—there is a temptation to allow glib assumptions to pass uncorrected, the more so because the view of history given by a railway museum, say, or a revived folk custom or an old-fashioned trade catalogue is bound to be a highly specialised one. It is the teacher's duty to round out these impressions. And this brings me to the final point I wish to make in this book.

History teachers—and, indeed, historians—have in the past not been noted for their honesty. They have too often presented a convenient or attractive picture of the past rather than an accurate one. But slowly and subtly, a change has been stealing over the teaching of history during the past few years. Some of us might wish that the process were less slow and less subtle, but there is no doubt that the more romantic phase of history teaching, even in the primary school, is coming to an end.

There are a number of reasons for this, but probably the most potent is that the teacher's and the child's views of the world have tended to come closer together. It would be impossible, for example, to go through in today's schools with the Empire Day charades which so many of us remember from our schooldays between the wars. The anti-hero tendency of our age enables us to admit that, on all the evidence, although Nelson was a great admiral he was also a particularly nasty little man. In addition, we seem at last to have broken the middle-class myths about history. As a result, fewer teachers these days want to encourage the detailed study of court costume, for example, and you see on classroom reference shelves rather fewer of those books of line-drawings of Hepplewhite chairs and Adam fireplaces.

It has now become permissible to admit that most people did not, in fact, sit down at long tables to feast royally off boar's head; or travel by stage-coach; or, if they were young women, sit about like the ladies in Jane Austen novels weighing up the eligibility of the local bachelors. Instead, while Saxon thanes (of whom there were perhaps a hundred or so) ate their boar's head, the other 99·9 recurring per cent of the population were attacking much more humble hedgerow fare; while the stage-coaches provided the major means of long-distance passenger transport, most people who had to travel at all (and as a matter of fact most people never went further than five miles from their birthplaces during the whole of their lives) went on foot; while the Jane Austen ladies were sitting mooning in their bow windows, most girls were having the course of their lives determined for them by being seduced fairly summarily under a convenient hedge.

In fact, for most people—and we are now becoming too honest to conceal it any longer—life was, by anyone's standards and certainly by our own, a kind of hell. The spirit of Church teaching about life being a brief pause between birth and death—'brief life is here our portion' —was accurate enough. For most people, life stank—literally. It was cruel and barbarous, even quite late into the nineteenth century as the passage from Tom Mann's memoirs quoted in Chapter 5 shows, in a way that makes today's social injustices seem quite trivial in comparison.

On another plane, it is now generally agreed that not all that was important in the past took place between such men as Pitt, Metternich, Machiavelli and the Fugger family. We have come to realise that it is only recently that politics and international affairs have become important to ordinary people; though no one today can ignore the divisions between the eastern and the western world, a large part of the population lived quite happily in complete ignorance of the Treaty of Utrecht or the Congress of Vienna.

It is a good idea, therefore, for teachers of history to look occasionally at the total picture of the past which they are passing on. Is the information they are giving, or encouraging children to find for themselves, honest? Is it relevant? If they are presuming—and, like most of education, this *is* a presumption—to suggest what it might have felt like to be a coal-miner in Victorian times, or an agricultural labourer in the depressed 1920s, or whatever, is the picture they are presenting accurate and fair? To some extent, this depends on the teacher's sources—and this is why the remainder of this book is taken up with a source list— but it is also dependent upon the teacher's bringing to the study of history the same kind of professional integrity that he would expect to exercise in other areas of the curriculum.

Source list

Let's make no mistake: the approach to history outlined in this book makes considerable demands upon the teacher, notably on the question of gathering source material. Very little material has been produced specifically for the junior/lower middle age-range outside the familiar 'information book' series on the history of transport, clothing and costume, and so on. I have omitted these from this list since almost every educational publisher's list includes series of this type, all of roughly equal merit. Beyond these, the teacher is largely dependent upon books for the CSE age-range and above, most of which must be adapted for junior school use. However, I have included a number of books which, although produced primarily for older pupils, are nevertheless suitable for younger children, often because of their pictorial content. Also included in this list are selected secondary school books which offer source material for the teacher's own use and adaptation.

To a great extent, this source list is a personal choice, particularly with the items of regional interest, but a diligent search of the local history shelves of public libraries, the lists of any local publishers and the lists of specialist publishers in the field of local history, industrial archaeology, folklore and so on will usually yield material of equal local interest. The comments on individual items are, of course, my own.

1. Background books for children

Past-into-Present Series by various authors, published by Batsford. An extensive series of over twenty titles written mainly for CSE course work but within the understanding of most top juniors. Each volume deals with a different aspect of daily life—e.g., *Transport, Home Life, Law and Order*—from early times to the present day. There are illustrations on nearly every page spread, drawn largely from contemporary sources. At the time of writing, this is without doubt the best series of its type.

History at Source by various authors, published by Evans. Collections of facsimile documents, specially bound to facilitate removal for display or group work. There are notes on each item. Topics covered volume by volume include *Children, Factory Life, Agriculture, Roads before the Railways, Entertainment* and *Medicine.*

Jackdaws by various authors, published by Jackdaw Publications. Collections of facsimile documents and other material packed loose in a cardboard wallet, together with background notes. Some items are rather flimsy and are more suitable for display than for everyday use. Topics covered in recent history include *Shaftesbury and the Working Children, Peterloo and Radical Reform, Winston Churchill, The Early Trade Unions, The Great Exhibition 1851, Women in Revolt : the Fight for Emancipation, Battle of Britain, Man and Towns, London's Peelers and the British Police.*

Wayland Picture Histories by various authors, published by Wayland Publishers. Particularly well-illustrated, large-size books with a fairly simple text though intended for the general adult reader. The illustrations are generally from original sources and are not familiar from common use elsewhere. Typical titles : *Parliament, Railways, Trades and Crafts.*

Local Search Series edited by Molly Harrison, published by Routledge and Kegan Paul. Ten or so titles designed specifically for use in school research projects. Readers are constantly referred back to their own researches, and the aim of the series is to fill in the background to their discoveries. A little stark and unexciting in presentation, but useful and authoritative sources of teaching ideas. Titles include *The English Home, Looking at the Countryside, The Town Hall.*

2. Background books for teachers

Sources of History by various authors, published by Macmillan. Designed as topic books for secondary schools, but many suggest study outlines which are adaptable for use with younger children.

It Happened Round Manchester Series by various authors, published by University of London Press. Five titles (at the time of writing) on such topics as *Railways, Canals and Waterways, Textiles,* related to regional history. Illustrations meagre, but the books are rich in anecdotage and will suggest many useful starting-points to teachers in the appropriate area.

David and Charles list. David and Charles are the largest publishers of transport histories, histories of industry and books on industrial archaeology. The titles are too numerous to quote here, but few areas of Britain are not covered by one or more David and Charles titles. Most public libraries have at least the titles with local relevance.

Studying Urban History in Schools by G. A. Chinnery, published by the Historical Association. An account of local history projects organised in the City of Leicester which contains useful ideas adaptable to other urban areas.

A Select List of Aids of Use in the Teaching of Recent History by G. R. Brooks is a valuable classified source list of films, books, visual aids and other material. Published by the Historical Association.

Victorian Cities by Asa Briggs, published by Pelican, includes studies of Manchester, Leeds, Birmingham, Middlesbrough and London.

The Discovering Books by various authors, published by Shire Publications. Inexpensive little books on a wide range of useful topics, including *English Customs and Traditions, Folklore in Industry, English Fairs,* as well as a number of regional county volumes.

Industrial Monuments in the Mendip, South Cotswold and Bristol Region, by Neil Cossons, published by the Bristol Archaeological Research Group, Bristol City Museum. Annotated list of sites in the area described.

Victorian and Edwardian Yorkshire from Old Photographs covers the period from about 1850 to Edwardian times. There are similar volumes on London, Scotland, Oxford and Cambridge. Published by Batsford.

3. Books on traditional culture

Folksong collections:

The Penguin Book of English Folk Songs edited by R. Vaughan Williams and A. L. Lloyd (Penguin). Words and music of 70 traditional songs.

Marrow Bones, edited by Frank Purslow (EFDS Publications). About 100 traditional songs, words and music, collected mainly in Hampshire and Dorset by the pioneer collectors Hammond and Gardiner.

The Seeds of Love, edited by Stephen Sedley (Essex Music). Words and music of over 100 songs.

Come Listen, edited by Ian Campbell (Ginn). An attractive school collection of 36 songs, words and music, with excellent background notes. See also p. 66 for its accompanying record.

Victorian Folksongs edited by Charles Chilton (Essex Music). A mixture of traditional and music-hall material. Words and music.

A Book of Ballads by Alan Bird (Longman). Texts only of 70 ballads.

The Idiom of the People and *The Everlasting Circle,* edited by James Reeves (Heinemann). Collections of texts only of songs from, respectively, the collections of Cecil Sharp and those of Baring-Gould, Hammond and Gardiner. In each case, there is a valuable introduction.

Ballads and Broadsides edited by Michael Pollard (Pergamon). A collection for school use of 48 songs, texts only, with notes and an introduction.

Children's traditional games and chants:
The Lore and Language of Schoolchildren by Peter and Iona Opie (OUP).
Children's Games in Street and Playground by Peter and Iona Opie (OUP).
The Festival Book of Singing Games edited by Mary Wilson (Topic Records).

Miscellaneous:
Six Mumming Acts by Alex Helm and E. C. Cawte (Guizer Press: EFDSS Folk Shop).
Five Mumming Plays for Schools by Alex Helm (Guizer Press: EFDSS Folk Shop).
St George and the Dragon and Punch and Judy, edited by Diana John (Puffin).

Records of Folksong:
A Merry Progress to London and Sweet Thames Flow Softly, The Critics (Argo DA46 and DA47 mono, ZDA46 and ZDA47 stereo). Two collections of London songs ranging from medieval balladry to modern pieces, with topics including Bartholemew Fair, the Great Fire, street cries, highwaymen, Dockland life. Full texts of the songs, with notes, are given in a leaflet enclosed with each record.
The Rout of the Blues, Robin and Barry Dransfield (Trailer LER2011 stereo). Mainly northern songs including *Scarborough Fair, The Tree they do grow High,* and a number of traditional dance tunes.
Waterloo: Peterloo, The Critics (Argo DA86 mono, ZDA86 stereo). Songs from the period 1780–1830 illustrating urban and rural life and the tensions of increasing urbanisation. A leaflet contains full texts and notes.
Ian Campbell and the Ian Campbell Folk Group (Music for Pleasure MFP1349 stereo). Twelve boisterously sung songs about navvies, transportees, beggars, firemen, agricultural labourers, sailors and recruits. Produced in conjunction with the song-book *Come Listen* (published by Ginn, see above).
A Yorkshire Garland by the Watersons (Topic 12T167 mono). Fourteen Yorkshire variants of mainly rural songs, mostly from the eighteenth century.
Deep Lancashire and *Owdham Edge* by various artists (Topic 12T188 and 12T204 mono). Lancashire songs and other material, including dialect items.

Folksongs of Britain Series (Topic). Ten records compiled from field recordings by traditional singers. Not all suitable for school use, but Volume 3, *Jack of all Trades* (12T159), Volume 7, *Fair Game and Foul* (12T195), Volume 8, *A Soldier's Life for Me* (12T196) and Volume 9, *Songs of Ceremony* (12T197) are recommended.

Seasongs and shanties by various artists (Topic TPS205 mono). Selection of sea-songs, mainly Liverpool-based, sung in rough, unprettied-up style with various accompaniments.

Blow boys blow, Ewan MacColl and A. L. Lloyd (Transatlantic XTRA 1052). Sea-songs and shanties.

Tommy Armstrong of Tyneside by various artists (Topic 12T122 mono). Songs and ballads of the north-east coalfields, late nineteenth century. (See Chapter 5).

Folksound of Britain by various artists (EMI CLP 1910 mono). Selection of instrumental music, songs and dances from all parts of England, recorded at a Royal Festival Hall folk-music festival.

The Watersons (Topic 12T142 mono). A mainly rural, mainly northern collection of songs, including many which survived in oral tradition into the present century.

A Prospect of Scotland, by various artists (Topic TPS169 mono). Variety of music and song, including pipe tunes and items in Gaelic.

The Sweet Primeroses by Shirley Collins (Topic 12T170 mono). Mainly rural songs collected in the south of England, including *George Collins*, *The Babes in the Wood*, *The Cruel Mother* and other items descended from medieval balladry.

Frost and Fire, The Watersons (Topic 12T136 mono). Seasonal and ceremonial songs.

The Long Harvest, Peggy Seeger and Ewan MacColl (Argo ZDA66–ZDA75). Ten records of traditional ballads in English, Scots and North American variants.

Steam Whistle Ballads, Ewan MacColl with Peggy Seeger (Topic 12T104 mono). Industrial folksong, mainly from southern Scotland, Lancashire and Durham.

Folk Songs, various artists (Topic TPS201). Mixture of rural and urban songs and ballads ranging from medieval origin to late nineteenth century. Specially selected for school use as a companion to *Ballads and Broadsides* (Pergamon, see above). With teachers' notes extra.

Fred Jordan (Topic 12T150 mono). Songs of a Shropshire farm worker, all learned by the singer from his friends and relations.

Bob and Ron Copper (EFDSS LP1002, available to EFDSS members and associates only). Songs of Sussex (See Chapter 5).

Other useful records:

Streets of Song, Ewan MacColl and Dominic Behan (Topic 12T41). Children's skipping and play rhymes and chants, linked with a rather tedious commentary. A booklet containing text and notes is enclosed with the record.

Children's Singing Games (Topic IMP-A101). Recorded at a festival of singing games at Redriff Primary School, Bermondsey, London. Thirty-three games sung unaccompanied but each prefaced by one verse of piano arrangement. Produced in conjunction with *The Festival Book of Singing Games* (Topic, see above).

The Knotty, a musical documentary (Argo ZTR125 stereo). Adapted from a production at Victoria Theatre, Stoke-on-Trent, presenting the story of the North Staffordshire Railway, 1835 to 1923. A mixture of dramatic excerpts, traditional and modern music, and field recordings.

The Age of Steam (BBC Enterprises 144 mono). Music and source material read by actors covering the period 1830–1880. Transcriptions from BBC schools television programmes.

Into the Storm (BBC Enterprises REB 39M mono). BBC Archive recordings from 1939.

Singing the Fishing and *The Big Hewer* (Argo). Transcriptions of BBC radio programmes incorporating traditional and new songs with field recordings. The subjects are respectively the fishing trade of the east coast of England and Scotland, and miners and their folklore.

Useful addresses

Publishers

Batsford, 4 Fitzhardinge Street, London W1H 0AH.
David and Charles, South Devon House, Newton Abbot, Devon.
EFDS Publications, 50 New Bond Street, London W1.
Essex Music, 68 Oxford Street, London W1.
Evans Brothers, Montague House, Russell Square, London WC1B 5BX.
Ginn, 18 Bedford Row, London WC1.
Historical Association, 59a Kennington Park Road, London SE11.
Jackdaw Publications, 30 Bedford Square, London WC1.
Longman Books, Burnt Mill, Harlow, Essex.
Oxford University Press, Education Department, Walton Street, Oxford.
Penguin Books, Harmondsworth, Middlesex.
Pergamon, Headington Hill Hall, Oxford OX3 0BW.
Routledge and Kegan Paul, 68 Carter Lane, London EC4.
Shire Publications, Tring, Herts.
University of London Press, St Paul's House, Warwick Lane, London EC4.
Wayland Publishers, 101 Grays Inn Road, London WC1.

Record manufacturers

Argo, 115 Fulham Road, London SW3.
BBC Enterprises, Villiers House, Ealing Green, London W5.
EFDSS, Cecil Sharp House, 2 Regents Park Road, London NW1.

EMI, Hayes, Middlesex.

Music for Pleasure, Astronaut House, Hounslow Road, Feltham, Middlesex.

Topic, 27 Nassington Road, London NW3.

Trailer, Leader Records, 5 North Villas, London NW5.

Transatlantic, 120 Marylebone Lane, London W1.

Index